I0014771

Stop the Data Madness!

Lessons from a Lifetime in Data Management

Merrill Albert

Technics Publications
SEDONA, ARIZONA

115 Linda Vista
Sedona, AZ 86336 USA
https://www.TechnicsPub.com

Edited by Sadie Hoberman

Cover design by Lorena Molinari

First Printing 2024

Copyright © 2024 by Merrill Albert

ISBN, print ed.   9781634624992
ISBN, Kindle ed.   9781634625043
ISBN, PDF ed.   9781634625067

This book is dedicated to the people open to exploring new ideas in managing data.

Contents

Introduction

Life revolves around data. Unfortunately, most people don't realize this and take data for granted. Without devoting the necessary attention to data, you risk everything based on your data. How do you expect to make good business decisions if you're basing them on bad data? How do you expect to get good reports, analytics, and Artificial Intelligence (AI) without good data?

This book will help you better understand and work with data. Yes, there will be some theoretical narratives, but there will also be many real-life examples. I see data all around me. Unfortunately, I also often find myself a victim of bad data. I know I'm not the only one, but many people might not realize that the issue they're facing is because of bad data. I might be more aware of it than others, but I hope these stories will help others realize what is happening behind the scenes and know how to fix it.

Someone commented online one day that data is a poor boss. I responded with, "Data's not the boss of me." That's a good way to think about managing data. We should work with data, but it's not the one in control. We need to be the ones in control. By managing our data, we can give it the attention it needs to be useful to us.

Don't be a Data Victim. Don't be a Data Offender.

Are you a data victim? Or are you the data offender?

You're a data victim if:

- You don't have the right data you need
- You don't have enough of the right data
- You don't trust the data
- You don't know where to find the data
- You don't know what the data means
- Different people interpret and use the data differently
- The right people in the company aren't making the decisions
- You don't know if there are any privacy restrictions on the data

You're a data offender if:

- You enter data in multiple places and it might not be identical
- You use the same term to mean different things throughout the company
- You don't get the appropriate input from people throughout the company in making decisions
- You don't have the right data, so you just make it up
- You use the data based on what you guessed it means, but you guessed wrong

---

Data in Real Life—Crimes Against Data

CrimesAgainstData has an origin story.

When I witness people misusing data, I call it a "data crime." This quickly progressed to me adopting the hashtag, "CrimesAgainstData," which you'll find attached to some of my posts on LinkedIn. Someone pointed out that it wasn't so much a crime against data as it was a crime against me! That is somewhat true, although not all stories I tell are personal to me. Some are stories I hear about from others. It might be more of a crime against someone using data.

Data crimes are unnecessary. Why do we have data crimes? Perhaps some people are being careless and are trying to do something quickly. Perhaps some people haven't been trained in good data principles. For the most part, people probably aren't thinking through how their actions might impact others. They don't realize how a little thing like data can have far-reaching implications.

Data crimes can be about people misusing data or people creating bad data. Data crimes can have operational or analytical impacts. If you don't have the correct address for a customer and a truckload of perishable goods can't be delivered and is wasted, your data crime has a huge impact. If gender is a missing data point on many of your customer records and you're trying to do analytics using that data, that data crime will impact your results and the decisions you make on those results.

Think through the implications of what you're doing. Do you have the right data to reach your customers? Do you make up data that might offend your customers? If you think bad data is statistically insignificant, have you proven that?

Why are all these data crimes happening? I think it comes down to education. Do people really understand how to properly treat their data? Data management requires some structured knowledge. You do not learn this from a one-hour seminar, a one-week vendor course, reading a book, or watching YouTube videos. Those can help give you a base to work from or reinforce your training, but you want to ensure you're not taking a narrow view of data. You need to understand the big picture.

One

Data Management

Just because you have data does not mean it is the right data.

Managing your data is work. You have to make sure that you have the right data on which to base the rest of your work. The people who are good at managing data are the same people who like having structure and disciplined processes that people will follow. This is not a free-for-all. Having a casual Wild West environment will give you data you can't count on. And if you can't count on your data, how can you use your data for reporting and insights? How can you sign off on financial statements as being accurate?

Without good data, you can't have good analytics or AI.

Data management helps create and maintain good data. Without data management, you can't guarantee good data. Worst case, you base business decisions on bad data you don't realize is bad. You better hope you find out it's bad before it's too late. Data management is a lifestyle or culture you build into your everyday work. It is not a one-time project. It is not about hiring a new team of people or filling out templates.

You'll notice in this book that I refer to "good data." Some people talk about "good quality data." I prefer the more inclusive "good data" because it's not always just about quality. You want more than just quality data. Quality is important, but so is knowing what the data means, if you're allowed to access it, if there are restrictions on what you can do with it, etc. Also, you might think you have a data quality problem, but that's just the way it manifests. You might actually have another problem, such as a metadata problem. For instance, your total number of customers may be wrong not because your customer data has quality issues but because not everyone agrees on how you're defining customer.

Storytelling goes hand-in-hand with data management because people often think of data management as esoteric. You need stories to make it come alive so people understand why it matters. Some people call these "use cases." I prefer "user stories" or "scenarios." The difference is that "use case" is a term that came out of technology and we need to stress from the beginning that data management has a business focus. Words matter. Use business language or real English words rather than technology-speak. Data is not the same as technology.

Purposeful Data Management

Data is used as the basis of your business decisions. Data is used in analytics. Data is displayed on reports. You can use tools to view data in databases. But how good is this data? Are you basing your decisions on good data or just a random set of values of unknown origin? Data management is the foundation that gives you good data. Without that foundation, you're just hoping you're using good data.

> *Reports, analytics, and AI—all need a base of good data to be successful.*

When companies are not following good data management practices and realize they need to, it is important to recognize the problems you're having that you can overcome. If you undertake data management because you think you should, or because it showed up on an audit as something that you were missing, you probably aren't going to get effective data management. You might get something, but is it what you need? Data management is not a "check the box" activity. Data management requires a purpose. Without the passion to get usable data, why are you undertaking it?

Some people who want to establish data management might be met with resistance due to a belief that the value isn't there. People with that attitude are probably trying to focus on the end result of getting some dramatic insights that transform the business into a financial powerhouse. The reality is much different. You aren't going to get to those insights without first having good data. You need to communicate that story.

To counter any resistance, you might need to establish a business case. In this business case, present why you need data management. Document the scenarios where there are problems because of poor data management. For instance, it is common for people to struggle with data issues while trying to create a report. I believe there is often a correlation between how high up in the company the person who needs the report is and how much extra time people will dedicate to that report. If the CEO needs a report and poor data is causing delays, people will work overtime and weekends to work through the issues to deliver the report on time. In this scenario, the problem is hidden from the CEO. When the CEO is then asked to devote resources to data management, the CEO doesn't recognize that there is even a problem to fix.

Data management is not something that can be done to you. You can't hire someone to take over all of your data management responsibilities. While there are some activities you can outsource, ultimately, it's your business and you own the business rules. You give direction, even if you use an outsourcer for some activities.

Data management activities need to become natural. You're building a lifestyle—a culture. When you use data or perform actions on data, you have to constantly think ahead of what your actions might mean in the future. Do you think the data is self-explanatory, so you don't document what it means, and will ultimately struggle at some point in the future trying to remember what it means? Do you ignore a data anomaly thinking someone else will see it and resolve it, only to have it fester as it transitions to other databases and eventually shows up on a report, but no one knows there's a problem?

Companies often don't recognize who has accountability over data. There is often a mistaken belief that the Information Technology (IT) department "owns" the data. Not true! It is easy to see how people come to believe that because they rely on IT to load data, download data, produce reports, etc.

Don't confuse the maintenance of data with the business rules themselves.

The business owns the business rules. They know what they do with the data. They know what the industry is doing. They know the regulatory rules. Don't expect someone with technical expertise to know all this.

There has to be collaboration between the business and IT, with both groups recognizing what the other brings to the table.

Also, don't expect to have a single person who knows all the business rules. Companies establish data governance organizations because they recognize that there has to be shared ownership of business rules. For instance, a customer interacts with many departments and you can't expect one department to know how every department needs to interact with that customer.

Companies often struggle to know how to start with data management when they haven't been following data management practices. The reality is that data management has been around since the beginning of data. Some people have been following good data management practices all along. If you haven't, data management becomes a daunting task. For instance, without business definitions, you may have to define hundreds or thousands of terms. No one can define hundreds or thousands of terms in a single sitting. However, if you haven't defined any yet, you are faced with this task. Take it in pieces. Define some. Give yourself a break. Define some more. Repeat. Repeat. Repeat.

Companies also often struggle with data quality. You can prevent data quality issues by following good data management practices. The longer it takes you to find and solve a data quality problem, the more time has been spent in making decisions on bad data. In a perfect world, you must resolve data quality issues when you receive or create the data. Ensure you have good data quality and you don't have to worry about it later. Ensure you establish some data quality health checks to see if you missed something. Many companies set this up before putting an application into production. If you haven't, it becomes another daunting task to address later. Again, take it in pieces. Establish some data quality rules. Monitor for problems. Resolve problems at the source so they don't continue. Then repeat.

Data management is a lifestyle. At no point do you declare that you're done. You might work on data management projects with consultants, but the end date of the project is not your end date of data management. You still need to keep things running properly in production. Even if you define all your terms and data quality rules, your data will change. New data comes along. Problems appear that you hadn't previously anticipated. You must continually follow good data management practices to avoid getting into that mess again. You got yourself out of it and don't want to put yourself back into it. You work yourself into a mode of managing and monitoring what you have, responding to new regulations, and onboarding new data. If you don't like "lifestyle," think of it more as a program than a project.

Foundation for Insights

Data insights start, naturally, with data. If you get the data wrong, your insights will be wrong. Who wants to take business actions on insights based on bad data?

> *If you've done nothing to build good data, why should you expect it to be good?*

The real problem is if you're reacting to data insights you don't know are based on bad data. You need to prevent that because you don't want to make incorrect assumptions. The data industry has been around for a long time and has proven techniques for building that solid foundation upon which to base your insights. Using these techniques and following a structured methodology provide the discipline needed to build that foundation.

Building the foundation takes time, but you need to take that time if you want the insights to be worthwhile. Don't try to cut corners. Don't, probably erroneously, assume your data is good and you can just start using it. Prove it.

One of the problems most companies face is that the business changes over time and the infrastructure needs to change with it. However, particularly in older applications, people often built inflexible designs that could only handle the business processes known at that time. As the business grew, offered new products, or partnered with other companies, the infrastructure needed to grow. Often, rather than taking the time to fix the infrastructure, people made compromises, sometimes for speed of implementation. Compromises don't typically age well. Eventually, you need to take the time to fix it. Going forward, learn from past mistakes and don't make those compromises.

Stick to your disciplined approach and don't implement something until it's ready.

Once you've got your foundation right, make sure it stays that way. When companies follow a disciplined methodology, they follow the steps to maintain that foundation. They'll avoid shortcuts and sloppy processes. Employees who will follow the steps to maintain this foundation are also important. Things can fall through the cracks, so you'll want to implement data health checks, such as a yearly review process, but for the most part, following a methodology will keep that solid foundation you need.

Once you have the right foundation, you'll have the right data you need to develop the insights that will move the business forward.

Combat Data Management

"Combat data management" is a term I coined for something you don't want. Unfortunately, it happens a lot. Ideally, good data management is in place, allowing you to easily create reports and perform analytics. If data management is not sufficient, you're faced with trying to work with substandard data. Maybe you're trying to use a particular data element and find there are multiple data elements called the exact same thing, but you don't know which one to believe. Maybe you're looking for data that isn't complete. Maybe you can't find the data. Maybe people at your company won't give you access to the data you need. Whatever the issue, these are data management problems you're now faced with when all you want to do is produce a report. You wind up having to solve these problems under pressure because you can't create your report until you fix these problems. You're in combat mode trying to fix your problems. You eventually get your report, but it probably isn't created with 100% confidence.

In a perfect world, you realize that you learned something from this and undertake an effort to implement data management properly. Unfortunately, this is not a perfect world. If you do nothing, you have relegated yourself to a continual process of combat data management. That's not a good place to live.

Data Management—How Far Have We Really Come?

We talk about the people–process–technology triad to manage data. Think back through the history of how this triad has evolved. The thing that immediately comes to mind is how much technology has advanced. When we think about the manual calculations performed by people like Katherine Johnson, how did we ever get something up in space so many years ago? But what about people and processes? Have they evolved?

For years, I followed a government process that included multiple steps and forms. Nothing was difficult; it was just tedious. At a certain point in the process, we had to perform a step that felt like it should have been one of the first steps in the process. When I questioned it, they admitted that it made more sense to be earlier in the process, but they seemed to have no way to fix it. The last time they went through a process improvement exercise simply resulted in more steps and paperwork being inserted at various points of the existing process to make it even longer. It made them want to keep the status quo and not question it further.

Processes are there for a reason and can help maintain sanity with data. Unfortunately, the processes are often needed to enforce common sense and save people from themselves. Compare it to the covenants of a homeowners' association. There can be some crazy-sounding things in some covenants (e.g., no windchimes, keep your grass cut, don't store non-running cars on the road), but you know those things are there because they created conflict at some point and someone wrote them up.

We're all in this together and need to work together.

Then there are people. It always comes back to the human element. You can throw as much technology as you want at something and establish as many processes as possible, but people can be unpredictable. Are they going to follow the processes? Will they use the technology? Will they follow a different path, thinking it's perhaps a better path? Will they go rogue? Data security always comes to mind. I remember a time sitting alone in a dentist's office with a computer screen and calendar in front of me. I had seen the dentist click on my appointment box and all my information popped up. All I had to do was click on one of those boxes and I had access to other patients' Personally Identifiable Information (PII). I assume they had established the applications as secure from outside forces, but they weren't secure inside the building. If someone is careless and leaves computer screens unlocked, you never know what will happen. And don't get me started on all the stuff you can see from fellow passengers on screens in airport waiting areas and on planes.

When we think about how people handle data these days, technologies have evolved. We've got software now where we used to be doing things manually. We've got software to replace the omnipresent Excel spreadsheets. Although, let's be serious—we still like our Excel spreadsheets. It's the tool that keeps on giving. And that's when you start thinking about how much has really changed. Buzzwords come and go, and sometimes all we do is put a new name on something old. Call it something else and you can attract people to the bright shiny object, thinking it's something brand new that will solve their problems.

> Chances are, the problems are more people- and process-related. If you haven't changed those, the technology won't help you.

I come from an enterprise-wide background. We built enterprise-wide solutions, whether for global companies or just a company within one country but multiple regions. We didn't think small. It always surprises me to hear that people are still building siloed applications. Why are people thinking small? Why aren't they thinking about building something to help more than just their immediate view? There can always be complications of different regulations in different countries, but don't we all have the same problems? Let's communicate. Why are so many problems rooted in the lack of communication? Sometimes, it's people trying to do things on their own and boost their egos rather than finding out what other people need and working together.

If you implement a new technology without any business involvement, what you'll solve is a technology problem. That's fine if what you have is a technology problem. But, if you have a business problem, you need to involve the business. That means the technology team accepts that they need to take the lead from the business on business problems, and the business team accepts that they need to take responsibility for knowledge sharing rather than thinking the technology team can read their minds. Again, it comes down to people communicating and working together.

Good data management practices, including data governance, have always existed and always will exist. It might not have started as an actual "discipline," but well-organized people started it because they felt this was the right way to do things. Those people are still around and now take a more formalized approach to data management. You might be able to throw more technologies at it, but you must follow good data management practices to succeed. Some people complain about bureaucracies and say people aren't "agile," but you can't circumvent good data management practices. You can work on improving processes to make sure they're efficient, but you can't eliminate the processes. Why do people think they can just throw more technologies at something and it will magically fix itself? Plus, technologies are always changing, whether improving or just being renamed (and re-sold) as the latest bright shiny object, so you have to keep buying more technology. Clean up your people and processes. Use good data management practices. Those are where you get the most benefit. Follow the data governance mantra of business-led but technology-supported.

> *Data governance is something you participate in, not something that's done to you. Let's learn from the past and not continue making the same mistakes over and over again.*

Industry-specific Data Management

I've seen some consulting companies try to develop data management from an industry perspective. They might have some people who focus on data management for the finance industry and some on the pharmaceutical industry. From a data management perspective, there's no reason to do this. Some have separated people between government and commercial. Data management is data management. You don't need to do it differently from one industry to another.

Think about data as an industry in and of itself. The data solutions you develop can apply to any "traditional" industry. Although there are industry-specific terms, data management is the same for each industry.

Cleaning Your Data Closet

You've cleaned your closets at home. But what did you do at work? Did you clean your closets there? I'm not talking about the physical closets where you keep the remnants of old technology and power cords that don't fit anything. I'm talking about your data closet. Have you cleaned up your data management and your data infrastructure lately? Organize your data. Set up a solid foundation of data management. That will set you up for success in the future.

Data archive, retention, and destruction

Clean your closet. You know the one. You've been throwing things into it for years. You've probably got some computer disks in there that kids have never seen in their lifetimes. You might have limited space and need to keep things in off-site storage. Now, think about your databases. Have you been accumulating data over the years because you think you might need it some day? Or maybe you just forgot to look at what's in there. You might even find a nice surprise and discover some very useful data you didn't know you had. You may have some data you no longer need and can archive or purge it. You might have to think about what data to keep where you have easy access to it, and other data that you can archive where you can still get to it but it might take a little longer. Maybe it's time to talk to legal and determine the rules. You might be surprised to find that legal is concerned about data retention as well as data destruction. Once data has reached the end of its useful life, legal will often tell you to get rid of it so it doesn't turn into a liability.

Data inventory and metadata

You look at some people's closets and everything is labeled. They've printed labels and stuck them to closed boxes so they can easily find things and don't have to open every box when they're looking for something. Now, think about your databases again. Have you got everything labeled? We use a term called metadata that provides key information about data elements. Have you inventoried all your data elements? Once you start examining what you have, you might be surprised at how much you have and how scattered it is. You also might find that you have different versions of it in different places, and then find that they don't match. Have you defined all those data elements? They're not always self-explanatory, especially to new people, and some terms can be so similar that you need precise wording to know the difference. What about data lineage? Sometimes thought of as "data genealogy," data lineage helps you identify where the data came from–identifying its parents, its grandparents, etc. Having the data lineage documented will help you if there's a data issue and you need to track back to the source of the problem.

Data quality

As you go through your closet, look at everything to see what to repair or problems to address. Maybe you have a pair of pants and the hem thread is hanging loose. Maybe a sweater has some holes in it. Maybe you have some suit pants and can't find the coordinating jacket. Maybe you've got two identical T-shirts because you forgot you had the one and bought another. Now, think about your data again. Do you have some missing data? Maybe you don't have a phone number for a customer, but you could really use that. Do you have the wrong data? Maybe a customer's address doesn't exist. Do you have multiple versions of the same data, and perhaps they're not identical? Now would be a great time to systematically review your data and fix the problems. However, it's important to remember that you must find the source of the problem, or you will be continually fixing data. For instance, you don't modify a phone number if it will be overwritten weekly by one of your processes, such as data coming in from a vendor. You certainly don't update financial information because it doesn't look right. Figure out where things went wrong and get it fixed there.

Data lakes and analytics

While you're at it, what about the kitchen junk drawer? You've got one of those too. It contains so much stuff that you can't find anything, so you keep buying new stuff. Your databases might have turned into the kitchen junk drawer. If you have a data lake, it has an even higher probability of being the kitchen junk drawer. Data lakes started with good intentions, but companies often placed such few restrictions on them that they became catch-alls. You could put anything in there, do some amazing analysis, and then realize you couldn't repeat it when you wanted to operationalize something. Unless you've followed good data management practices, you'll probably have difficulty proving your results, leading to people mistrusting your results. They might want to believe you, but how can they decide on the results without proof?

In summary

Data management helps you control your data to provide the right data to the right people to make appropriate and timely decisions. Cleaning your data closet is part of that. Invest some time in it now, and you'll be better prepared to address the future.

Building Your Own Data Function

If you haven't been concentrating on data and then realize you need more focus, perhaps because you have some bad data or need that data as input to your analytics program, you might be confused about where to start. The key is starting with data governance. That gives you the foundation to build all other data management capabilities (e.g., metadata, data quality).

In establishing data governance, you'll identify a cross-functional team that will be involved in data. You need this cross-functional team, not a single individual. Think about who uses customer data. It's essentially everyone at the company. Would you rely on one single person being able to speak for the entire company on customer data? You really need to bring in those different perspectives, such as marketing, sales, operations, customer care, risk, etc. The customer data that one department needs may differ from the customer data that another department needs.

> *Data governance is not an IT function. Yes, IT keeps the applications running and maintains the databases, but what they do is based on what the business tells them to do. Think of data management as business-led and technology-supported. Both groups need each other to work together for the success of the company.*

Data governance itself isn't difficult, but it can be difficult to start. The problem is that there's no template to fill out because you're building a data culture that has to fit in with your business culture. Your data governance organization will look different than someone else's. There's also a lot of noise in the industry. How do you weed out the bad data governance information from the good? Working with a consultant to get this set up and prepare yourself for success is often helpful. A skilled consultant will be able to pick through the noise and help you get this established.

A data culture means you will have people throughout the company thinking about and valuing data. If you're maintaining data correctly from when you receive or create it, it will be ready for you when you need it. The thing you want to avoid is attempting an analytics project with bad data. If the data analyst or data scientist has to spend hours, days, or weeks resolving data issues, you haven't done your job. Data skills are different from analytics skills, so you can't expect your analytics staff to be able to resolve data issues successfully.

Once data governance is in place, you're ready for other data management capabilities. For instance, you wouldn't want to tackle metadata without data governance in place. How you define something like "customer" could differ in each department, so you need to reconcile those different perspectives to have a company-wide definition of "customer." Data quality is the same.

Quality in one department could be different from another, so establish data governance first as your foundation so you've got the people you need.

Outsourcing is something that some people think about because outsourcing IT operations is a common practice. There are definitely IT tasks that can be outsourced. However, if we go back to the earlier mention of this being business-led and technology-supported, the company has to maintain ownership of its business knowledge. This cannot be outsourced. However, the company can work together with an outsourcer to give guidance on what the outsourcer should work on.

Some companies use a "steward" job title. While that can be helpful if used properly, it's important to understand how to use a steward. When we think of what the word means, we should really all be good stewards of the data, not just a single person with the job title. If you have set up data governance properly, at best, the steward is bringing up issues to the rest of the data governance organization. The steward is not empowered to speak for the entire company. Additionally, a steward is not a full-time position. I often avoid the job title to reduce confusion.

Lastly, there's analytics. If you've properly managed your data, it will be ready for you to use for analytics. While analytics are different from data, there are similarities. You can govern analytics because something you want to use for the entire company might need input from different business departments. You can define analytics because once you create them, you probably want them documented so you can replicate them in the future. There are parallels.

Managing data is not something that should be difficult. The issue comes when you haven't followed good data management practices and then try to retrofit a solution into chaos.

You need to build a culture of thinking of data first. Don't wait for it to get bad and then try to fix it later. That's when the duct tape comes out and you MacGyver a solution.

Maturity Models

Maturity models can exist for numerous things. You might have a data management maturity model that lets you evaluate how your company is progressing with data management. This will cover all data management capabilities. Other maturity models could be more specific per capability, such as a data governance maturity model. There are commercial maturity models out there. You can work with a consultant who has a maturity model. Some have four levels. Some have five. Basically, you have to find what works for you.

Maturity models help you evaluate your company practices. Some people love them because it helps them understand where they are and where they want to be. Other people don't love maturity models. Some people misunderstand the reason behind them and worry that they're being evaluated and criticized, or that their jobs might even be in jeopardy. That's not the purpose at all. A maturity model does not evaluate people—it evaluates processes.

Ideally, the end result of a maturity model evaluation is more than just a number. Is there a huge difference if you're a 2 or a 2.2 out of 5? Aside from that number, what you want is an understanding of what went into that number and what you need to do if that is not where you want to be.

Beyond an evaluation, education is an unexpected benefit and possibly even more valuable than a number. Some people are doing a maturity model evaluation because they're in the early stages of data management or don't understand why they're having problems with data management. By going through the maturity model, they learn the things that they're being evaluated against, which also means the things that they need to do to build a more successful data management function.

Maturity model levels can be numbers or names. Use whatever the client is most comfortable with. Some might refer to "level one" or "reactive." Some people might be uncomfortable being told they're "reactive," so they're more comfortable with an innocuous number. Others might be uncomfortable being told they're a level one when they know there are five levels.

> *Communication is important so participants understand you're not there to hurt them.*

I've met people who want speed with maturity models. Can we just get this done in a day or an hour? Can we just hand out a list of questions and fill it out ourselves? You can do how much or how little you want, but I think the purpose of a maturity model is to benefit the company more than just checking the box that you did a maturity model exercise. If I handed out a list of questions and asked people to fill it out, they likely wouldn't understand, particularly if they're new to data management. If I got in a room with twenty people and ran through a bunch of questions, I would get a collective response. Some people would be more vocal than others. Some people wouldn't agree with the group but would be afraid to speak up. Some people wouldn't understand the questions but would be intimidated to ask in front of their co-workers.

I've found that a maturity model works best in a one-on-one environment. I go through each question with people so they understand it. We take the time to go through examples of things they might have seen, which help them understand the questions. Even if the end result is a low number, it's a win when we come away with that level of education. I have practically heard the lightbulb go on when someone finally understands why there are so many issues getting accurate reports. If we think of the maturity model as education, it comes across as more valuable when the participants have been involved instead of sitting through a boring lecture. They're often engaged and you have established a number of people in the company who understand more about data management and want it.

User Story—Two Data Analysts with Different Data Management Experiences

Two data analysts were roommates. They had similar jobs but with different companies. They often shared what they were doing at work over breakfast, demonstrating the difference between good and bad data management.

One morning...
I got this great assignment at work yesterday. The big boss came and asked me if I could use my "fancy analytics," as he calls it, to predict possible loan defaults. If so, they want to take action to prevent that from happening.

Wow! I got the same assignment at my place! We've got some good tools and I've been told that I can ask for other things if I need them.

Me too! There are so many flashy tools out there these days. I've attended some seminars and I want it all!

I'm going to slow down and see what I have to work with, but it's nice to know that I have that support.

Another day...
How's your project going at work?

Pretty good. Everything's going smoothly. We've got all the data I need and the analysis is going well. I'm working with some of the business people, and they were really surprised by the details I could give them. We're focusing in on some problem areas. How about you?

Things aren't going so well. I was so excited to work on this, but I kept getting all these errors. It turns out that we don't have all the data. I don't understand why. We've got these loan files, but some of the data columns are blank and we really need that data. I've been pulling paper copies out of the archives to see if I can recreate it. It's really tedious.

We don't have those problems. IT produces these data quality reports for us. Whenever there's missing data, it shows up in a report, and people work with the business to identify it and fix the problem. I've heard everyone talking about "root cause," where they figure out where the problem started and fix it there. Maybe there was an issue with the input program or something they brought in from a vendor.

Another day...

What's new today with your project? Did you get all the data you needed?

I think I got most of it. There were a couple of things I couldn't find, but I was able to make it up.

Make it up?!

I compared it to other loans and looked at what we did have. I think it's good enough.

Ok—it's your job! That might not be the best approach though, if you had a regulatory report you were working with.

We'll be fine.

Another day...

What's the latest?

I discovered something really weird yesterday with ZIP Codes. Some databases store it in 5 digits, and some use the zip-plus-4 configuration. I guess that's not a big deal, although I don't know why it has to be different. I noticed some of the ZIP Codes were only a length of 4, so I looked into that a bit more. It seems that it's sometimes stored as numeric and sometimes character, so I think there are times when the leading zero gets truncated.

So what did you do?

For everything with a length of 4, I just add a leading zero when I process it.

Are you sure that's ok? Is it maybe just the "plus 4" that you have? Did your business stakeholders approve that business rule?

I didn't ask anyone. I just did it. I'm sure it's ok.

Didn't you already say that about making up missing data?

Another day...

What's happening in your world? You've got all the data now, right?

We have data in every column, but we still have problems. I've been comparing these two data sets and I'm expecting to see some similar numbers but they're not the same. How can something like that happen?

That seems to be pretty common as companies grow. They don't seem to take the time to build the data architecture properly. We've got something called the "single source of the truth." It means exactly what you think it means. I can go there and know I'm getting the right data. I don't have to search different databases and try to determine which value is right.

I wish we had that! I've been running around the office talking to people who keep sending me to someone else who might know what the truth is. This is crazy!

Another day...

I hate to ask, but what's happening now at work?

I thought I had it all worked out, but then I discovered another mess. We've got this column called "loan type code." You would think that's pretty simple, right? It turns out that I can't figure out what the right set of values is. Depending on where I look, I get different values.

We've got a "loan type code" too! We have a central repository I can go to to get all those values. All the applications use the same values. It seems straightforward.

We need that! I was trying to figure out the right set of values, and everyone told me that Sheila knew them. It seems they changed the values over time and didn't update them everywhere. The problem is that Sheila retired last year. People still call her, though. I tried and it turns out she's on a cruise. Won't be back for another couple of weeks.

Another day...

Did Sheila ever get back to you?

She did. She had a great time. She gave me the values. I wrote them on a post-it and stuck it on my cube wall so I won't lose them again. I'm sure I'll need them in the future.

You think so? Can't you fix the databases? That sounds like the root cause of a lot of problems.

That will take too long. We'll just keep the post-it. We'll be fine as long as I don't lose it.

Another day...

Is anything new?

I had to call Sheila again today.

Oh no! What happened?

She's enjoying her retirement but has so much knowledge of what's happening with the data. I suspect we might bring her back as a contractor. I couldn't figure out the customer addresses because there were differences. She told me that there could be a different address each time someone buys a new product. There's no central address anywhere! She told me Rudy had a way of pulling it all together.

Who's Rudy?

He's retired too. But he built this database to bring all that stuff together and everyone loves it.

Is it kept up-to-date?

They don't know! It just runs in the background. I get the feeling everyone's afraid to touch it and potentially mess it up. They use it, but I think it's held together with a hope and a prayer.

Another day...

What's happening with your project these days?

I've been so frustrated. I went and talked to Joe in IT operations. I told him that I was expecting them to give us good data and that I kept seeing problems. He told me they used to be better but keep having these acquisitions. They have to take over another company really quickly and they don't have time to bring the data in correctly. That's causing a lot of problems. He tells people that they need to fix things, but no one seems to have time. They just assume he's got it together with all his late nights, but they aren't sharing all the business rules with him. I think he just feels lucky when he's able to read their minds and get the right data to them, or at least what he thinks is right.

You've got a lot of late nights too!

That's true. The quality of this data is killing me. They don't realize what I'm going through to get the results for them.

Another day...

Is there anything new?

I discovered something crazy yesterday. I've been analyzing different data sets by matching "customer ID" in one database with "customer number" in another database. I assumed they were the same thing, but I was getting odd results. I took a better look and realized that it was a bad assumption. It sometimes means the same thing but sometimes different, so I wasn't doing the analysis correctly.

I know you said you didn't have a central repository with code values, but are you saying that you don't have one for just general definitions either? That should have resolved it.

That would have been nice. I guess I shouldn't have assumed either. I also discovered that they once needed another column and it was easier for them to repurpose a column they weren't using anymore rather than change the database and add a new column. So, I now have to compare it to this other column that has a really bizarre name. No one ever would have guessed that one!

That's rough. They never would have allowed us to do that at school. The teacher would have marked that wrong for sure. Did you ever buy more analytics tools?

We didn't. We realized that the data wasn't good enough for analytics. We would just have been throwing away our money. I was really looking forward to it too.

Another day...

What's the latest?

I made a huge mistake this week. I was comparing data in these two different data sets. I asked someone a question and she told me that one of the data sets comes from a vendor and there's a contract telling us what we're allowed to do with the data. Apparently, we're not allowed to bring it together with this other data set like I was doing. The vendor calls it "reverse engineering." I really screwed up.

No one told you? I had to go through training on what I was allowed to do with the data before they gave me access. They're trying to prevent getting a fine from the vendor. I hope you don't have to pay up!

Another day...

I haven't heard much from you lately about that project. What happened? Did you ever get it done?

What a disaster! We had to scrap it. I'm so disappointed. Every time I asked a question, people started realizing that the underlying data wasn't good enough for the analysis. They decided that since they couldn't trust the data, they weren't going to be able to trust whatever analytics I was able to come up with. I really disappointed the boss.

What does that mean? What are you doing now?

My day is made up of analyzing data sets and identifying

problems to fix. I didn't go to school for this! Analytics was supposed to be fun. We've got a room full of people fixing data all day long. We run reports, fix data, and then do it again next month. It's a never-ending process. I guess that's how you make your job secure! What about you? I was so caught up in my own problems that I didn't ask you what was happening with your project.

I had a different experience. We could count on the data, and the project was successful. I was able to give results to people almost right away and they worked on taking action. Everyone was happy with what came out of it. I've worked on other projects since then. They also invited me to attend some of their data management team meetings. From what I hear, they were experiencing some of the same problems you had before they got better organized. This team really has its act together. They have processes in place so they get consistent results. They have metadata centralized, so you can easily look up what something means and determine its data lineage. They know who makes decisions and they take the time to fix the root cause of problems.

We haven't had to call someone like Sheila!

Funny. Sheila has been a life saver! It does sound like you're working in a good environment. I'll have to ask them tomorrow if they know about this data management stuff. Was it expensive?

It doesn't seem to be because it's not a technology-driven thing, so there aren't expensive tools to buy. Everyone's talking about their "data culture" and "living the data lifestyle." I've been pretty impressed at the questions I hear people asking. They seem to have it together.

That does sound nice. By the time I was able to get some data together, it had taken so long that everyone forgot what the original question was that we were trying to solve. And that included me! I need that data culture.

O Data

Apologies to O Christmas Tree, but I came up with a fun way to talk about data management.

O data, O data
What crimes have you committed?
O data, O data

Whatever happened to you?

We had high hopes. You started well.
Then someone clicked into Excel.
O data, O data
Whatever happened to you?

O data, O data
What crimes have you committed?
Who shared you? Who deleted you?
Oh no—here come the lawyers.

How can I operate with you?
How can I analyze this mess?
Who put you in production?
You clearly were not ready.

O data, O data
Where is the missing data?
I really cannot trust you
To extrapolation.

Who mastered you? Oh—nobody.
You thought you did not need it.
O metadata. I need you.
I really don't know what you mean.

O data, O data
You really need some management.
I trusted you. You let me down.
Whatever was I thinking?

You really need some governance.
It really is quite simple.
O data, O data
What crimes have you committed?

Data in Real Life—We Lost the Weapons

Kathleen Hicks, the US Deputy Secretary of Defense, was being interviewed by Jon Stewart, an advocate of veterans' rights. He was concerned that there was fraud within the Department. She was trying to explain how it wasn't fraud. She said, "We don't have an accurate inventory that we can pull up of what we have where."

What we have here is a classic data management problem. You didn't keep track of your data, but now you're trying to find it. Except in this situation, some of that data represents large expensive equipment. Some of it can be deadly. And they have no idea where it is.

Keep track of your data from the beginning. That way, you'll never be involved in a hunt to find out where it is. In this case, that hunt essentially involves equipment that could be anywhere in the world. No one wants to admit they lost it.

Data in Real Life—What the 2020 Census Tells Us About Data Management

I call myself a "data person." Professionally, my data career started with a Bachelor of Mathematics degree from the University of Waterloo, and I have worked with data ever since. I was probably born this way. I see statistics in the news and question whether the data they used was appropriate. Data is what it's all about. When you can't trust your data, you can't trust the analytics generated from that data. Worse, you could be gleaning what you think are amazing insights, only to discover later that these were based on flawed data. That could lead to bad business decisions and/or public embarrassment.

How do you get your data right, and how do you define "right"? You need to prevent problems from getting into your data. If problems creep in, you must fix them as early as possible. The longer you leave problems in your databases, the more time and money it will take to fix all the areas the data has permeated.

I work in the field of data management, which is a discipline in and of itself. We take care of data through careful management, decision-making, and implementation.

But explaining data to people can be difficult. Unless you turn it into a story, data can sound too theoretical. This is the story of the 2020 US census.

A tale of two addresses

One day, I received my census form and filled it out online. Six weeks later, I received another census form. I took a closer look.

Every census address has a unique ID, and this form had a different ID from the earlier one. It was my address, but it was slightly different. One of the words in my address was "Captain," and one of the versions had abbreviated it as "Cpt." I lived in a metropolitan area that had two valid city names, and these forms varied in that respect. For instance, mail going to "New York City" and "Manhattan" will get to the same place. Although different, they were both valid addresses for me.

Throughout my career, I've seen so many companies struggle to reconcile addresses. It shouldn't be that way. The USPS publishes standard abbreviations. Software is available to automate the standardization, such as turning "Captain" into "Capt." The Census Bureau doesn't seem to have done this.

Some people might think this isn't a big deal. "So you got two census forms in the mail. Toss one out," you say. But wait–this error has implications. The US government uses census information to determine the number of seats in Congress. They use it to determine funding for schools, roads, and public services. Family history researchers will use it (in 72 years). I'm sure I'm not the only person who received multiple forms, but we don't know the magnitude of the problem. It may not be significant, but we won't know unless we look further.

A human problem

What went wrong? Many people will blame it on a "computer problem." The computer didn't cause the problem. A human caused the problem. We just don't know which human.

When we follow good data management practices, we talk about data governance. When we're properly governing our data, we know where the decision rights lie. People throughout the organization collectively use their knowledge to make decisions. What happened here?

Perhaps lists of addresses came from multiple sources that had to be reconciled into a single list. To do that, you define business rules to bring those addresses together. You need to know that "Captain" and "Cpt" are the same. You need to know that two city names refer to the same place. In data management, we refer to this as Master Data Management (MDM). We want to get to a single source of the truth.

In the case of the census, were the business rules properly governed so the right people made the decisions? Were the business rules shared with the programmers and tested to demonstrate that they were programmed correctly? These are problems caused by people, not computers.

The ramifications of bad data

Data quality is a huge part of data management, and we need high-quality data for the census. We must test before releasing into production. Many organizations don't give the care they should to testing. If Census Bureau employees had properly tested the business rules, data, and programs before sending the census forms, they would have found the error that showed up in my mailbox. Census officials could have stopped it earlier when it was cheaper to fix. The code could have been reprogrammed, retested, validated, and then sent. Doing all this could have delayed the census, but it would have been accurate. Now we're dealing with the problem and its implications.

The majority of people who got multiple census forms aren't data people like me. If it happened to you, you might ignore the additional forms. You'll remember that you have already completed your form and will just throw out the new one.

However, the Census Bureau doesn't recognize it as a duplicate address. Their records show that you didn't fill out your census form. You will continue to be hounded with forms in the mail until they finally send a census worker to your home. Not only have they spent additional money to send you extra forms in the mail, but now they're spending money on census workers. They need census workers in any case, but depending on the magnitude of the problem, they may need to hire more. And since the 2020 census occurred during a pandemic, repeat visits are expected because people don't want to open their doors to strangers.

Another possibility is that you will fill out a second form, forgetting that you already did so. Perhaps you have multiple people in your home, and you didn't realize that someone else already completed it. The Census Bureau receives that information, and one of two things happens next. They are double-counting people if they don't realize that some people received multiple forms. This can easily skew numbers, affecting public services and representation in Congress. If, on the other hand, they realize they're double-counting, they will have to go through the forms and remove the duplicates.

But are they really duplicates? In many cases, they are. Households don't change too quickly, so if the forms are filled out accurately, they will match (except for that address problem). The census, however, spans a period of months, so it is possible that people moved, were born, or died during that period. Those two forms for that one address might actually wind up having different results. Does the Census Bureau then try to reconcile them? Or do they just accept the chaos of their results? Applying this concept to your business, you can see how finding a data problem too late in the process will cost you time, effort, and money to pull yourself out of the quagmire.

There's yet another option. Ignore the issue. If you have a population of 1,000,000 and send multiple forms to 100 of them, that number might not be significant enough to act on. If multiple forms go to 100,000, that might attract more attention.

So, you need to understand the implications of bad data. Depending on your needs, you might need perfection in your data. Is it a life-or-death issue? Is there a threshold you'll accept if you don't require perfection? If the problem extends beyond that threshold, what happens next? If the overall business decision is to move ahead with some bad data, is there a subset of people who will be adversely affected by that decision? If so, will you need to communicate with them?

The bigger picture

Being my family's genealogist, I also think ahead to what the data errors in the 2020 census mean. In 72 years, family history researchers will have access to this census data and they'll be trying to make sense of it. What will they do when they see their ancestors listed multiple times? What will people think about how the 2020 census was conducted? Will people trust it?

What about history? I stumbled across a problem with the 2020 census. Unless the Census Bureau's programs got recoded for 2020, it's highly likely that prior censuses were also wrong. That means the government's decisions based on prior census data could also be inaccurate. We'll likely never know.

Although I've told a story about data with the 2020 census, all decisions have their own data story. People generate analytics and then derive insights from those analytics, but they have to make sure that there are people taking care of the data first. Without good data, there's no point in continuing with analytics. A well-managed data environment, however, will take you far.

Two

Data Lifestyle

D ata management is not a one-time project. While you might undertake a project to implement data management or a project to implement part of data management, the truth is that it's not over when the project is over. Think of data management as a lifestyle.

Many companies do not follow good data management practices and then undertake a project to do so. The reality is that it should not have come to this. Data management has been around as long as data has been around. If companies have not followed good data management practices, they have created the environment they're working in. There can be reasons for this. Sometimes, companies start small and don't think they need data management. By the time they get successful and really need it, they have a data mess that needs to be disentangled. Other times, inexperienced people are hired who don't understand data management and the value it brings. They may mean well and think they're working in the best interests of the company, but we have the data specialty for a reason.

Some companies build a data management team before they really know what they need. I'm more in favor of first hiring your data leader, perhaps a Chief Data Officer (CDO) and having that person, with knowledge of data management, establish the team that's right for the company. Otherwise, you risk hiring a bunch of people you don't need or don't need yet, and don't know how to utilize.

Do you need an entire data management team? Maybe not. If you have a team, make sure you clearly document the roles of each person. It might be sufficient to have that single data leader acting as the data management expert to build out the data management capabilities at the company. For instance, would it make sense to have a metadata expert? That might be someone you need temporarily to help get metadata established, but you should not have a single person defining all your metadata.

The business people using the data are the ones who know the data and understand what it means, so they need to define it. They likely need guidance to pull that information together and properly define metadata, but it comes from the business and not a single individual.

> *Whenever I hear people talking about having a huge data team, I worry that they went down a data rabbit hole and are working in isolation separate from the business.*

Data Literacy

Data literacy became a buzzword. Then people started saying that the opposite is illiteracy, and we don't want to tell people they're illiterate! But it's also been pointed out that there are different levels of literacy—not just literate and illiterate—which can make it ok.

If you're trying to bring data awareness into your company, use the words that matter. If people want the latest buzzword, use data literacy. If that word turns people off, use something else. You don't want to turn them away from the message because they can't get past the title.

So what do I use? I had to think about that a bit. I'm not new to educating people about data, but "data literacy" became a new term. I think I've just been calling it "data education." I'm not a big fan of creating new terms for something we've been doing all along. It doesn't seem to help.

Comparing data management to something people can relate to can be helpful to start that awareness. One comparison is to tax season.

I can hire a tax accountant, but I'm still responsible for giving her all my documents, answering all her questions, making decisions when I'm given options, and validating the end result to ensure I didn't forget to tell her anything. I don't have to be the tax expert, but I participate in the process.

You can look at data management the same way. You can offload some tasks to people, but you still maintain the responsibility of providing everything they need to do their tasks, answering their questions, making decisions, and validating results. Everyone doesn't have to be a data management expert. Not everyone needs weeks or months of heavy training. You might just need to provide streamlined education for awareness so people can be supportive. No one person needs to take on everything alone. I once worked with a company that thought they could outsource all data management and maintain no oversight. That didn't end well.

Three

Data Governance

Data governance involves people, process, and technology.

The most important part of data governance is people. People are responsible for making sure that the right people have the right data and information to make appropriate and timely decisions. Processes are important so you understand the tasks you need to perform and you can follow them consistently. Technology is the last part of data governance. Many tools on the market can assist people and processes in managing data. Think of the technology as the accelerator. You can still do the work without it, but it probably makes things go faster.

I often say people, process, and technology—in that order.

Data governance involves a cross-functional team of people who work together to provide timely and accurate information to support business decisions. You will need to build a data governance organization. This does not mean hiring a bunch of people. This means building good data practices in everything you do. It means collaboration. It means working with other people to make decisions based on the complete company perspective, as opposed to having to decide on your own without all the information, and risk making a wrong decision.

Without data governance, you risk having someone make a decision without all the information. People might make decisions that work for their individual departments but not for the company as a whole.

Can your business exist without data governance? I don't think so. Without data governance, you go one of two ways—the Wild West or a dictatorship. The Wild West would be everyone doing whatever they want regardless of how it impacts others. A dictatorship would be one person attempting to speak for everyone, regardless of what the data means to each department and what they need to do with it. We don't want either the Wild West or a dictatorship. You want the value you get from data governance.

Data Governance is the Starting Point

You can work on data quality. You can work on metadata. However, data governance is required for data quality, metadata, and all other capabilities to succeed.

In data governance, you're establishing the decision rights over the data. You're identifying the people who will be involved. Those people will be involved wherever you're governing data. If you need to look at the data to see if the quality is right, or if you need to determine how the company defines and uses a certain term, you need the people for that. Get the people in place and you're setting yourself up for success with the other data management capabilities.

In data governance, you're bringing people together. You're not working in isolation. The people working with the data work together to get the company data used correctly and yield trustworthy results. There's a huge people component. When I say people, process, and technology, in that order, it's because the people component of data governance needs to be in place first.

That doesn't mean establishing data governance and taking a break before doing something else. You've built momentum and can't take a break. You need to be ready to start tackling your data problems. With data governance in place, you have the right people to handle your data quality problems. Without data governance in place, starting with data quality might mean getting together a ragtag group of people with good intentions but not the knowledge and authority to tackle the problems.

Growing up, my after-school job was working at the library. Due to construction, we had to move the contents of the library. Multiple times. The first time, professional movers were hired. Over the weekend, they got everything from point A to point B and got all the books on the shelves. I guess they did what they were contractually obligated to do. We came in after the move to a disaster. Dewey Decimal System anyone? We couldn't find anything and neither could our patrons. After significant work like a Tetris puzzle, we got it organized. After that, all moves were done by the employees who knew where the books belonged. It was all about having the right people, not just any people.

> *Data governance has the overarching reach of all the company data and the means to make impactful decisions.*

Data governance is where all the data management capabilities come together. I like working in the space because of how much it can benefit the company.

What You Choose to Govern can Shape the Success of Your Data Governance Initiative

I believe you should govern the management of your data, which is also consistent with some people calling this a "data management" or "information governance" program.

If you govern the management of your data, you're looking at things like master data, data quality, metadata, data architecture, data transformations, data privacy, data archiving, data retention, data destruction, data access, etc. Basically, if the word "data" is linked to it, you should govern it.

The more you govern, the more impactful data governance will be. For instance, data quality that isn't governed means you fix quality once and then it goes bad again. Metadata that isn't maintained and governed goes stale.

Also, look at your geographical focus. A global reach can have more impact than localized solutions because there's more of an opportunity to consolidate data.

If you build a solid foundation of governed data, the analytics, reports, AI, etc., based on that data will be trustworthy, repeatable, consistent, and defendable. Don't build on a squishy foundation.

Build a program, not a one-time project.

Data governance is everlasting, not a one-time project. You build an organized structure of people, process, and technology to support the processes and applications that acquire, organize, distribute, and use data. You're defining how to manage the decision rights and accountability over the data to derive the most value from it.

This does not mean removing people from their jobs. It means embedding data governance into their day-to-day activities. The only full-time data governance people may be the ones acting as leaders guiding others in using the right data to provide accurate and timely information to support business decisions.

People involved in data governance need to understand the vision. They need to know where to head, their role, and their impact on the business. They need to understand what's in it for them. That will allow them to be advocates. Without knowing the vision, they're just doing a task and probably waiting for it to be over to get back to their regular jobs.

Work on data governance holistically.

Implement a new application and include data governance, data quality, MDM, etc., as part of the design. That builds everything together. However, if you have a data governance program but not data quality processes, you could say you will develop a data quality program and build elements into your data governance initiative.

Once people start accepting data governance tasks as part of their jobs, it will grow organically. For instance, once people realize others care about getting the data right, they will raise potential data issues. If they see a potential data quality problem, they will bring it to the group rather than just accepting it. If they don't understand a term, they'll bring it to the group to come to a common understanding.

If you have regular data governance meetings, a great thing to discuss is the projects that need data. When a project is kicked off, do the participants understand the data they need, how to access it, what it means, and pitfalls to avoid? Can someone attend the project kickoff to help them get their bearings? During the project, are they finding data issues that need to be resolved by the people working in data governance? Syncing the projects with data governance will benefit the company. Some companies do this through a Steering Committee, although some companies aren't ready yet to bring data into their established Steering Committee. If the data governance lead does not hear about data issues from the project teams, you can assume they don't understand data governance. I have yet to find a company with perfect data.

Build a sustainable infrastructure

Some people might implement an MDM tool and then decide they need data governance. It should really be the other way around. Involve data governance through the life of the MDM project and into implementation and operational processes. The people involved in data governance can define the business rules to follow when designing the master data rules. Other people might be involved post-production in keeping the integrity of the data intact. Governing master data is a great place to start, but it's not the place to end. If you just govern your master data, you're missing out on the potential of the rest of your non-master data.

If you decide to govern metadata, you can build off your successes there to further develop data governance. If you have a data-driven data architecture with more code table-driven programs than hardcoding, you need to ensure that you have the right codes defined. That would happen through the people you have involved in data governance. The problem with just defining metadata is that people see it as a one-and-done initiative. They define the metadata and then move on to the next thing. People need to understand where data governance is going because metadata might be updated over time.

Data quality is a great thing to govern. Build this into your designs. Ideally, you don't want to bring data quality problems into your databases. If you generate your own data, you can place controls at the application level to prevent bad data from coming in. People involved in data governance can identify what is acceptable data and what is not. If you get data from outside your organization, you have less control over its quality. In these cases, you need to decide if you're willing to accept any data issues and still bring in the data or if you want to reject some data and get it fixed. Regardless, you should implement periodic data quality health checks to check the data quality in your database.

Business-led and technology-supported.

This is a business-led initiative supported by technology. Technology supports the business needs, but doesn't lead it. IT people can be very knowledgeable in implementing an application but don't always have the business background to make the business decisions. For instance, regarding data retention, IT might be focused on keeping as much data as possible accessible. However, Legal might focus on ensuring data is kept as long as legally required and then purged.

Data governance can be difficult at first to focus on because some people think of governance as a technology capability and don't understand that governance needs to involve non-IT people for business rules, but it is supported by IT people to implement solutions. For instance, the business people might not know or care about designing a data architecture that is data driven instead of database driven, but they can clearly respond when you talk to them about specific rules or codes that are needed. Use language they can understand.

Don't constrain governance

If you narrowly focus your data governance initiative, you will have narrow results. For the biggest impact, you need to govern the management of your data. If resource constraints restrict your focus, at least let people know where you're going, how you'll get there, and when.

Data Governance versus Data Management

Some people use the terms *data governance* and *data management* interchangeably. They are different. Data governance is one of several capabilities under data management. These capabilities work together to manage your data.

Since "governance" can be scary to some people, I often talk about building a data management organization rather than a data governance organization. They are performing data governance, but I'm good with it if it makes them feel more comfortable by calling it a data management organization.

Also, you're governing the other data management capabilities, so I don't feel calling it a data management organization is much of a stretch. The actions are the same, even if it has a softer name.

For simplicity, I have referred to it as the "data governance organization" throughout this book. However, I have found in practice that people are more comfortable calling it the "data management organization."

> *Think of data governance as the heart and soul of data management. Unless you start with data governance, you won't be successful with data management.*

The Data Governance Diet Versus Lifestyle

When I teach people about data governance or help a company implement data governance, I talk about it as building a lifestyle. You don't do your job and then reserve the last hour of your day for "data governance activities"–you incorporate data governance into the day-to-day activities you do. I also talk about it as a "program" not a "project."

Think about dieting. Experts always say that dieting doesn't work. Sure, you might go on a diet and lose some pounds, but when the diet is over and you return to your regular habits, those pounds return. What works is if you change your regular eating habits. You develop a new lifestyle. The same is true with data governance. It's not a project you do and then return to your ways "before data governance" at the end of the project. If you haven't changed processes and how people think about data, what was the point? You haven't built the data governance lifestyle.

People always ask me how data governance will help them. It depends on what they're choosing to govern. Your impact will vary from that of some other company because you might govern different things. What you're governing helps you focus on the lifestyle changes you need to make. It's not one size fits all. If you're implementing data governance without understanding your goal, you'll never know if you're successful, so you probably won't be.

I worked with a company that had a huge data-sharing issue. They had multiple contracts to acquire data from various companies and each company let them share data with contractors, provided that they got permission in writing. If they didn't get permission, they were in violation of their contract, which had various repercussions. Sharing data was easy to do. An employee downloaded data to an Excel spreadsheet and emailed it off to someone. There was a violation if that someone wasn't an employee and they hadn't asked permission. By bringing data sharing under data governance, we were able to have processes and policies around sharing. We were able to educate people on the processes and the repercussions. It became natural for people to stop and think before they hit "send" on their email. We certainly had to stay on top of it, particularly with people who didn't regularly share data combined with a constant stream of new hires. However, for those who did this regularly, asking permission became a natural part of what they did.

Data acquisition is something else we can govern. I was at a company that empowered people to buy the data they needed, leading people to buy whatever they wanted, particularly towards the end of the year when they had budget money left. They didn't think about who else could use the data. They weren't interested in sharing. They had a singular focus on what mattered to them and the fact that they had money to get it. By bringing this under data governance, we brought a more thoughtful approach to thinking about data and being good conservators of company money. When a company acquires lots of data from other companies, if they don't keep track of it under data governance, they quickly lose track of it. Another department might already be buying that same data set, and trust me, a data vendor is more than willing to sell you the same thing twice. The company might already have a similar data set sufficient for the research. Or, there might be other departments thinking about the same thing who are willing to share in the costs of the data. You might also uncover a data set that is better than what you currently have and can switch vendors.

What about the companies that don't go on a diet and don't change their lifestyle? Unless they're the rare company that did it right the first time, they're probably in a slow decline and won't realize it until it's too late. At that point, they'll look for a data doctor to get them out of their mess. Maybe it's a plastic surgeon with a little tweak here and a little tweak there, or maybe it's a major overhaul. One company had an idea of doing "passive data governance." When I asked them what that meant to them, they knew they had bad data and didn't want to affect anyone, so they decided to leave things as business-as-usual, with the addition of a weekly cleansing process that resulted in a weekly manual fixing effort. Since the data wasn't fixed at the source, bad data kept coming in weekly and getting manually fixed weekly. Not a great career builder for that person who had to repeatedly fix the same data week after week! When I explained that their "passive" data governance meant "no" data governance, they decided they were ok with it. It was a shame because they had staff willing to fix data at the source and capable of fixing it at the source. Not to mention all the money they gave consultants week after week to do the manual work.

Ultimately, governing data comes down to a mind shift.

People often focus on the technical and the tools, but they can't help you if you haven't built the data mindset. The flaw is usually the human element. Humans can often be unpredictable. You need to find a way to make that mind shift and then keep it top of mind, which could be through things like education, regular communications, or posters around the office.

Data Governance—A Bright Shiny Object

I once sat in a get-to-know-you meeting when a company started a lengthy project with a consulting firm. We went around the room saying why we were excited about starting this project. A number of people from the company said, "Because we're getting our data put into the cloud!" They had no idea what that meant. They had a lot of problems, but not being in the cloud wasn't one of them. They had heard a buzzword, a bright shiny object, and thought they needed it.

I've spent my entire career working with data. I've seen things come and go and then sometimes come back again. I've seen new names being given to things we've been doing all along. What is consistent is that people get distracted by the latest buzzwords in the market. They don't think about what it really means or how it will benefit them. Maybe it's a form of ADD. Maybe it's FOMO. Maybe it's good sales reps?

The problem is that if they always jump at the latest buzzword, they probably will miss opportunities. Most companies don't have well-designed data environments. If that foundation isn't there, anything put on top of it has a high risk of failure. It's just like building a house. Build a house without a foundation and what do you have? At best, a shack that blows down in the first storm.

Data lake. Analytics. Data science. Machine learning. AI. Insert buzzword here! Just make sure that you have your data foundation nailed down first and then you can jump into those initiatives.

Garbage in–garbage out. That was a phrase that seemed to start in the 1960s, although a version of it was 100 years earlier than that with Charles Babbage. Unfortunately, it is still true today. If you have bad data, your results generated on that data will obviously be bad. I am always baffled at how companies want to spend tons of money on things like data science initiatives when they have failed to get their data house in order first. And now we're seeing the same thing happen with AI.

I've spent years working with data. I learned good data management practices at university. It was commonsense to do some of the things I've done. Although, I think some people are more geared towards orderly data environments and others are more geared to stuffing it all in a data lake and assuming someone will be able to do something with it. I've had people coming to me with a data lake asking what's in it, which is hard to figure out after the fact. If they did it right the first time, they would have a useful data lake.

You'll get what you need if you have a data governance program governing the management of your data. You'll have the right people in the company making accurate decisions about the data. You'll understand what you have and where you have it. You'll nail down what data quality level you need and ensure you get it. You'll master what needs to be mastered. You'll protect the privacy of your data.

It's time for many companies to take a step back. Figure out where they want to go. And then figure out if they have the data infrastructure that will help them get there. If they don't, that must be the bright shiny object they latch on to. Get your data house in order and move on to greater things from there.

If Data has Value, It Needs a Chief

What is the relationship between data governance and the CDO? Can data governance be successful without a CDO? The CDO role has been gaining in popularity. But you don't hire a CDO in search of a problem because it's fashionable and you're jumping on the bandwagon–you hire a CDO because you need a CDO.

So, can data governance be successful without a CDO? As someone who has spent my entire career working in data, I like to think we always need a champion in the form of a CDO. As someone who has sometimes worked as a consultant, I say, "It depends." Some smaller companies can be successful without a CDO. Some larger companies can also be successful without a CDO. In those scenarios, the data governance lead must have the appropriate authority level to affect change. Essentially, data governance and the CDO merge. Maybe the data governance lead gets called the data governance officer. If the data governance lead doesn't have executive-level input, it is likely the company hasn't realized the true value of data and is not data-driven.

From a purist standpoint, data governance manages the decision rights and accountability over data to derive the most value. This includes organizing people, process, and technology to support the processes and applications that acquire, organize, distribute, and use data. Data governance is part of a data management program. I approach data governance by saying that you get the most impact by governing the management of your data. From that standpoint, you're governing metadata, data quality, data privacy, data retention, etc. If you can put the word "data" in front of it, you should govern it. Looking at it that way, you're governing things that would fall under the CDO role. You're almost treating the data governance lead like the CDO without the title. However, does the data governance lead have the authority to make impactful decisions? The data governance lead often does not, which is where the CDO comes in.

Without a CDO, what decision-making power does the data governance lead have? Does the data governance lead give input to data acquisition decisions or merely react to what the company decides to acquire? Do employees have the power to acquire whatever data they want, or does the data governance lead provide a sanity check, perhaps identifying that similar data is already being acquired? Is the data governance lead hiring (or providing input to hiring) staff to report on data quality and operate the databases, or just trying to work within someone else's structure? You want someone responsible for providing high-quality data to your data scientists so they can generate insights from useful data. Is the data governance lead involved in decisions around how to strategically use data within the company? Is the data governance lead developing the data management strategy and roadmap, or is that held elsewhere in the company? Most importantly, is the data governance lead overwhelmed by operational activities, so there is no time to devote to strategic planning and decisions?

Often, it is essential to position a CDO at the executive level to have the right power and be the champion of policies and regulations.

I've heard someone say that if data isn't an asset of the company, it's an expense, and you want to be getting something of value. If data has value, it needs a chief–the CDO. What value does data provide to your company? Is there value in the data because you are selling or leasing it to other companies? Or does the data bring value internally? Do you need trustworthy data as a basis for reports and analytics?

Where does your CDO sit? I think a lot of companies, once they realize they need a CDO, create the role and insert it someplace within the existing organizational structure, often where the biggest data problem exists. They might put it under Finance, Regulatory, Legal, Compliance, or IT. They might think it doesn't matter where the role goes as long as they have it. That can be a starting point, but isn't typically the best place to land long term. Some companies realize that the CDO needs to report directly to the CEO, on the same level as other Chiefs. You might have to disrupt your organizational structure and shift reporting responsibilities. You need to be brave enough to set the CDO up for success. Don't go through the trouble of creating a CDO and then positioning the CDO incorrectly. Too many fail without the correct support.

Who is your CDO? The best CDO is someone who can blend business and IT, which is a typical data governance role when someone governs all aspects of data. The CDO needs to juggle both worlds by communicating with both and being an interpreter to bring them together and help them understand each other. With too much of a business focus, the individual might be unable to embrace the technologies that can help. With too much of an IT focus, the individual might be too tool-focused and implement tools without configuring them with the appropriate business rules. You need someone who has grown up with data, lived data, experienced the problems, and is passionate about getting the right data into the right hands to benefit the business. A data person is often born that way.

Data Governance—Business Versus Technology

I was once part of a data governance networking forum where we discussed different topics, such as where data governance fits within the company. Overwhelmingly, everyone agreed it was a business and not a technology initiative. However, some people recognized that there were difficulties in getting acceptance. Data governance involves collaboration between the business and technology teams, and both sides need to recognize and respect what the other brings to the table. The problem seems to be more about staying in your own lane.

> Data governance needs to be business-led and technology-supported. I've seen this over and over again. The question is really why this keeps coming up for debate.

From a business perspective, they must recognize that they own the rules and make decisions. They are experts in the business. They know the business goals and objectives. They know their constraints, whether through their industry or governmental regulation. They know the deals they have with suppliers and what those agreements allow them to do. They also have to recognize that the technology team has the skillset to technically implement those rules, ensure that the right data comes into the databases, handle this data appropriately, and monitor for data problems. The technology team can support the needs of the business and bring issues to them.

From a technology perspective, they need to recognize that they are neither business experts nor are they expected to be, and their role is to technically support the business. Also, they need to be forceful and speak up if the business is not providing the necessary help. I have seen business people think they can give the technology team very little input. The technology team can try hard, but they need that input, and the technology team needs to understand their role in the organization. Too often, they try not to let anyone down and mistakenly do things they shouldn't. I've seen technology teams make up data because they thought they should, when they really should have notified the data governance lead that there was missing data or new data that didn't conform to existing rules.

Some people think since "data governance" has "data" in it and data lives in databases, the technology team supports the databases, so the technology team must own data governance. So wrong! Don't be confused about where the data is stored. Besides, storing the data is pointless if you're storing the wrong data or doing the wrong things to it. Focus on the information the business needs, which is the business's responsibility, and then have the technology team store that information for you in the form of data.

> *Knowledge of business concepts and business direction is not to be confused with knowledge of where the data resides and how good the quality is.*

I've heard some people use a plumbing analogy. Think of the technology team as supporting the pipes and the business team as supporting what runs through the pipes.

Some people approach data governance from the standpoint that it doesn't matter where it fits in the company as long as you have it. That is a standard argument that people use on a lot of things, not just data governance. What typically happens is that it doesn't matter until one day when it does. That's what you're trying to avoid.

> *The business has to take responsibility for being the decision makers and driving it with the help of the technology team supporting them. The technology team has to take responsibility for technically implementing the business needs.*

They both have to play a role in testing to make sure to implement things correctly. I've seen far too many efforts like master data implementations where the business wasn't involved in validating data tests and then were shocked one day to find there were data problems. It becomes an even bigger issue when many companies move to outsource their technology operations. When that is done, the business needs assurance that this external team still understands their needs and is operating correctly.

I've seen companies decide to create a data governance organization and put a technology person in charge because they think that person understands data, has been with the company forever, and is a good career move. However, knowing how data is stored in a database is not the same as knowing what it's supposed to mean and do from a business standpoint. People often fall back on what they're comfortable with, and a data governance organization led by technology often has more of a focus on fancy tools than the more important people and process side of data governance. That means that the tools are overshadowing the true business needs.

> *Taking a technical approach can solve a technical problem, but data governance is not a technical problem.*

Staying in your lane is important. My career started as a logical data modeler where I worked with the business to understand the data, built a model, and then worked with the DBA to implement the design. The DBA was interested in a high-performance database. I was more interested in making sure that the concessions made in the implementation were not violating business rules. This type of thing happens a lot. The technology team might be concerned about making things run fast, but if that speed impacts accuracy, the business should be aware of it.

Establishing a business-led data governance organization can also have challenges by proving value. Especially in the beginning, there can be some concern if people are planning and not producing results immediately. It's about storytelling. Tell a story about what the problems are and how you're going to make things better. The stories need to be very specific to the company so people will understand them. Maybe the CFO is signing off on financial statements that can't be trusted because of poor-quality data. Maybe developers are working crazy hours dealing with bad data because they don't want to let down the CEO, who needs some reports. You might need to create a business case, of which I've written many.

> *Your data governance organization needs to be business-led and technology-supported. Collaboration between the two groups is needed for the most benefit of the company, with recognition of what each group brings to the table. Each group has unique skills that complement the others, and each group has to recognize the value of the other. Solve the business problem and everyone benefits.*

Ownership

Now that we've talked about data governance, let's clarify ownership. If you've set up data governance properly, you understand the concept of shared ownership. You've developed this team of people working together to make decisions. There's no one single person who owns something.

Despite that, some people still think they must find a single owner for everything. I don't know where that idea originates, but I encourage you to dismiss it. Ideally, you have some sort of data governance lead who is guiding the team through all data management tasks, but even this person doesn't "own" the data. At best, you can say that person owns the responsibility for working with the data governance organization to accomplish the tasks.

Who owns the data? That's a loaded question! When I started my career in logical data modeling, we worked with many business people on the model. We didn't have the concept of "owner" and didn't miss it. Then it became a field in the modeling tools and we strove to get a single owner per entity. That didn't always work well. Then, we realized it was easier to do at the attribute level. That worked better, but there were always anomalies. Sometimes, you would think about where it was created and try to make that department the owner, but then people in other departments heavily dependent on the attribute didn't like hearing they weren't the owner. You might consider who the main user of the attribute was, but that always made other users unhappy. So, you brokered deals. Maybe you had a little rogue spreadsheet on the side with the "company-official" owner and then the other people you would talk to when something came up about that attribute or entity. Clearly, many people had a stake in many data elements, and we weren't handling them well. But then along came data governance and it solved the issue.

With data governance, it's not about a single owner. It's about a group of people working collaboratively. Sometimes, the company even decided to call this group the "business data owners." I still encounter people trying to find that single owner. They haven't understood governance yet and the power it brings.

Customer data is another part of that loaded question. Does a company own the customer data? Do customers own the data about themselves? Many companies try to develop relationships with their customers. They want to understand their customers better in an attempt to better market to them and build their business. Does that come from taking whatever customer data you can get from whatever questionable source you can find? Probably not. Often, companies are giving customers access to their data online with the ability to change it. And that's what you want. Customers who want to do business with you are also customers who want to make sure that their data is accurate. For instance, don't call me male or we won't be doing business together.

Then, there's the customer data that the company sells. Many customers sign up with a company, perhaps to get discounts with the company, and agree to terms without reading them. What have they just agreed to? Over time, companies are updating these terms. More and more, the terms include what the company is allowed to do with the data. Maybe the company will use the data to better market to you, which you might want anyway because you like their products. Maybe the company will send the data to another company to do things with that you don't want done. Cambridge Analytica, anyone? You might have mindlessly agreed to the terms because you wanted a discount and then have to deal with the consequences, followed by changing your agreement to the terms. If customers have the right to change their data or ask for it to be changed, it shows that the company has recognized that they are not the pure owner of the customer data.

Aside from the customer issue, many companies debate whether the business or IT owns the data. My mantra with data governance is that it's business-led and technology-supported. It's not about single ownership. It's important to think about the collaboration between the two groups, but at the same time, everyone needs to stay in their lane. Recognize what each team brings to the table and work together for the success of the company.

> Asking who owns the data is the wrong question. The business owns the business rules. Technology owns the implementation and monitoring of those business rules. One without the other doesn't work. Don't confuse ownership of a rule about a data element with accountability for a business process acting on that data element.

A good example of ownership comes from a website that crowdsources gravesites. Helpful to family history researchers, people can look up grave locations, see photos, and gather historical information. People living near cemeteries can volunteer to take photos and upload them. Each entry has an "owner." If people see incorrect information, they can share that with the owner as a potential update. If the owner loses interest over time or is no longer maintaining entries, updates don't get made. People can get around this by creating a new entry for the same grave–duplication, which data people dislike. There's seemingly no governance over this site. If you request duplicates be merged, the business rule is that the first one in wins, so the owner never changes. While it might have started out as helpful to a family researcher, it becomes impossible for a family member to correct information.

Data ownership can be a tricky thing to think about. You need to understand what data is being discussed and what people want to do with it.

> *Overall, we have to rethink how we talk about ownership. Many people are asking the wrong questions. We need to think more collaboratively.*

Stewardship

When you work with data, some people use the term *data steward*. I'm not a fan of that title, but I will use it if a client finds it valuable and has already socialized that term. I think that whatever titles you use, you need clearly defined role descriptions. If you can clearly define what your data steward is going to do, then by all means, use the title *data steward*.

> *"Steward" is a real English word. If we consider what the term "steward" means, we should all be good stewards of the data. That should be in all job descriptions! If we're all acting as good stewards, does it make sense for anyone to have a job title of data steward?*

Some people have data stewards who concentrate on a particular capability. For instance, there might be a metadata steward, but what does this person do? Is this person writing business definitions? That's not an isolated activity. It really isn't the job of one person, and it has an end date when you complete all the definitions. Ideally, you write these definitions when you create your data model. One person may write them as a starting point, but then they have to go for review, discussion, and approval by the data governance organization. Once everything in your data model is defined, your task isn't complete. A company isn't static and will eventually need more metadata, but that should not be a 40-hour-a-week task. If you fail to create your definitions with your data model or fail to create a data model altogether, this task will need to be completed. Ideally, I see this led by the data governance lead. However, if that person is overworked, it can go to a metadata steward with the understanding that the task is to manage the creation and approval of all metadata. You might create a project to get the work done, but is there enough metadata work to do when the metadata steward has to wait for people to be available to review and approve definitions? Also, once the work is complete, what does the metadata steward do? It's not a sustainable job.

Similarly, some people have data quality stewards. Again, what does this person do? Is this person writing data quality rules? Like metadata, this isn't an isolated activity. It really isn't the job of one person, and it has an end date when you complete defining all the data quality rules. Ideally, you create all your data quality rules before something goes into production, so you're completing this incrementally. If you fail to do this and are playing catch-up, you ideally have this task led by the data governance lead working with the data governance organization. Maybe your data quality steward is monitoring data quality or writing data quality reports. Is your data quality so bad that someone needs a full-time job doing that? That would be sad. That means you need to spend some time fixing your problems. With so many tools out there these days, automate monitoring and then concentrate on the more important tasks of resolving the issues.

I have sometimes seen MDM stewards who monitor the MDM queue for data that falls into the error queue. Like other stewards, this shouldn't be a full-time job. If you make it so, you likely haven't set up good MDM rules and need to revisit them.

If you find yourself in a place where you think you need stewards, think of them as the people who lay the groundwork. They can do all the up-front work to help facilitate discussions with the decision makers in the data governance organization. You don't want to give your decision makers a blank sheet of paper. You want to make effective use of their time.

If we don't have stewards, what do we have? I'm a proponent of integrating tasks into existing roles. Creating your definitions and rules needs to come from the data governance organization. Monitoring and resolving data quality issues must also go through the data governance organization. If you have separate stewards, they're all going after the same people in the data governance organization, and those people only have so much time to give. You don't want to create a full-time role where stewards are waiting around for time with the data governance organization. Creating reports and other technical tasks need to come from the technical team. You could hire more technical team members, if necessary, but you don't really need a report writer in a separate data team removed from report writers in the technical team. You can easily keep those skills together for cohesiveness.

Data Governance and the Closet Analogy

You put things in your closet in random places. Eventually, you realize you're wasting too much time looking for things, or wasting money buying a duplicate of what you can't find, and you need to do something. You hire one of those closet cleaning/organizing services. They do a great job. It's a thing of beauty. They leave. You have not changed your behavior and it eventually happens again. You hire the company again. They realize they have a repeat offender—um, customer.

Compare that to your data. If you don't constantly take care of it, you don't know what's in the murky depths of your databases and whether that data is trustworthy. Some companies have built isolated data teams. The business has not changed any behaviors and expects that data team, who they rarely talk to, to get them out of any mess.

> Stop the madness! It's about building a culture. If you understand your data and constantly treat it well, it will treat you well and you won't have to panic when a lawyer or regulator comes knocking on your door.

There's a precursor to the closet analogy. You've let it go and now you've hired professional closet organizers to fix your mess. Then reality sets in. The professionals can do a lot, but it has to be under your guidance. If not, they won't know that the old item of clothing they think should be tossed is actually a precious vintage family item. Data governance is like that. You must retain your responsibility

DATA GOVERNANCE • 81

when working with the professionals so you'll get what you want and need.

Stealth Data Governance

Some people have used the term "stealth data governance." It's not necessarily ideal, but it can be a way to get things done. Some people really get scared of the term "data governance," so keeping the term out of it but still getting tasks accomplished can be beneficial.

With stealth data governance, you need someone skilled in data management. This person needs to lead people through data governance without them realizing they're involved. Questions can be asked of stakeholders without them realizing they're participating. Discussions might drag out for a long period of time as this person learns more information and might have to revisit conversations with stakeholders.

The problem with stealth data governance is that it's inefficient. By not addressing data governance head on, you risk not involving the right people or having people make decisions without being fully informed of all the facts.

An easier approach is to just address the issue directly. People aren't as delicate as some think. If the issue is that people are scared that data governance means bureaucracy, then don't use the word "governance." I've had better luck telling people we're building a "data management organization" than a "data governance organization." They're going to do the same tasks because I know the difference between data management and data governance, but if it makes it easier on them, then let's approach it that way. You won't be successful if you don't get buy-in from your stakeholders.

Essentially, "stealth data governance" is what we unknowingly did before the term "data governance" was invented. We needed things done and answers to questions, and we knew who had those answers. We brokered deals and kept notes. Eventually, the industry caught up with us.

Data Governance Enables Analytics

I've seen people blur the lines between data and analytics, not understanding what they mean and not understanding the skill sets needed. There are similarities but also differences. There are some distinct but complementary skill sets. Analytics needs data governance to be successful.

Today, a lot of companies are hiring Chief Data Officers. That person might be responsible for data and analytics, but from an operational perspective, it may be too much and too detailed for anyone. That Chief Data Officer may have direct reports of a data governance officer and an analytics officer. These people can work very well together. The data governance officer is responsible for all the company's data. That means the data is coming in correctly, understood, and properly used. The analytics officer focuses on the insights generated from the data and is often very statistically minded. The analytics rely on the data being correct and the rules of the data being documented and shared.

Good analytics techniques applied against bad data will yield bad and untrustworthy results.

I've worked with a variety of companies that used analytics. Some had analytics pushed down to a low level. It meant that people at a low level had the budget to work on analytics and the responsibility to pick the projects they felt were appropriate. One benefit of this was that people enjoyed having that level of accountability. Unfortunately, it often led to a Wild West environment where people were not consulting with others, sharing information, or ultimately making effective use of company money. I've also worked with companies that conducted analytics "projects," and there was oversight of these projects. The oversight wasn't highly bureaucratic, although people who like the Wild West probably didn't think so. The oversight was to make sure that people were communicating and conducting meaningful projects that benefited the company. Creative people can sometimes come up with similar theories, so with project oversight, we often found several people trying to do the same thing. By working together, they could share resources and possibly share some slightly different thought processes that would help generate even better outcomes for the company.

I've seen analytics project oversight built into governance organizations. I've seen data governance and analytics governance as separate organizations, but I've also seen them as the same organization. Whichever way you do it, the important thing to remember is that the analytics team needs good data from the data governance organization. The analytics team needs to understand what the data means and how to use it properly. The analytics team needs to understand data constraints and legal regulations. Often, analytics people are excited about the next big thing they can come up with, so someone needs to be there to make sure they understand the data they're using. In some companies, analytics people have been using the data for years and fully understand it. You need to make sure that's true, because people sometimes make erroneous assumptions based on unfortunately named database columns. In other companies, it can be helpful to have a project kickoff to an analytics project where someone representing data governance can explain what the data is, where it is, how to get it, how to use it properly and compliantly, cautions in using it, and potentially what to do with their analytics.

The result of an analytics project may be that an exciting conclusion has come up. You need to communicate this. You take on an analytics project to achieve a result that benefits the company. It should not be thought of as the latest bright shiny object to work on, and then you move on to the next bright shiny object when you're done. Promote your outcome, share the results that others can benefit from, and take the credit you deserve.

Planning for Records Management Success

Records management can fall under different areas of responsibility in a company. It might fall under someone with a library background. It might also fall under information management or data governance, especially when records are so digital these days. And if you're lucky, you get a data governance person with a library background. Oh wait–that's me! My first job in high school was working at the local library.

Records management needs someone highly organized. You need a place to store the records, you need a plan to categorize the records so you can retrieve them, you need to think through your strategy around retention and destruction, and you probably need to change behaviors so people actually use the repository.

Repository

Identify where your records will be stored and what tools you need. With so many records digitized these days, we don't always need those rooms full of binders anymore. However, there may be some paper documents that are required. Your records management strategy needs to consider all the necessary regulations and plan accordingly. Most people use the terms "structured" and "unstructured" data. Unstructured data, in my opinion, is typically only useful once you give it some structure. That structure comes through finding a manner to catalog the data so you can retrieve it. People often think of it in terms of "keywords" or "tags"–words that you can search for to help you find the records later and identify the document's physical location.

When creating the repository, you also need to consider where people will access the records. You might be able to have a centralized repository. However, some global companies implement decentralized solutions if there are restrictions, such as certain records not being allowed to leave a certain country.

Implement the appropriate security over your repository. You might be using a tool that allows you to secure each record separately, identifying who can access which record. If your tool has limited security, you will rely on processes and oversight to avoid inappropriate access to records. You might consider overseeing why people access certain records depending on the sensitivity.

Retrieval

Retrieving your records is the most important thing. You don't want your repository turned into the kitchen junk drawer where you know you have it, but you just can't find it. Determining how you will need to retrieve your records means working with the people who will use the records. The worst thing you can do is think of implementing a records management tool as solely an IT implementation. Like most tools, you need IT support to implement the tool, but you need the business to define the rules to configure the tool. The business will explain how the records need to be retrieved so the tool is configured correctly. Without the business explaining the rules, someone will come up with a retrieval mechanism that may or may not meet the user's needs.

Remember to think about flexibility when you plan your retrieval strategy. I've seen my share of applications where someone thought the users would only need something like a maximum of three different keywords to find the records. That is often shortsighted. Even if people start out saying there are only a handful of ways to access the records, that could change as they start using the records management application and seeing what is possible. If one of the categorizations is department, that works fine until the company reorganizes and creates different departments. If your application is too restrictive, you might implement another new records management application in short order.

It's never pretty converting your records from one application to another.

Retention and destruction

Determining your strategy around how long to keep records might be as easy as determining what regulations you follow and what your lawyers say. Lawyers often tell you to keep the records as long as legally required and then get rid of them. That has allowed people to realize they need to change their original strategy of keeping all records forever. They have realized that there are times when they want to make sure that "extra" records are not available if there are legal proceedings in the future.

Another part of the retention and destruction strategy might include archiving records, especially when you have a large number of records to store. For instance, there might be a need to keep records for ten years, but only the most recent three years need to be easily accessible. If the users can accept waiting a bit longer to retrieve the later seven years of records, those records might be archived somewhere. Just don't turn the archive into the kitchen junk drawer and forget what you put there.

Repository usage

Getting people to use the records management application is sometimes the most difficult of all. Some people will be frustrated at how they are trying to retrieve records without it and embrace it immediately. Other people will be skeptical of it and avoid using it unless they have to. This is where you need to step in and change behaviors.

> People don't usually like it when others tell them what to do "just because." You need to explain why you're doing it and how it will benefit them.

Tell the story to build passion about records management, or at least interest. What was the business case behind implementing the records management application in the first place? Some companies have specific reasons for records management. It might be as simple as having an easy place to find the records and sharing information. When the records are easily accessible, you can quickly get them and then get on with the real (and exciting?) work you need to do. What you want to avoid is people squirreling away the records on their hard drives and then they get lost when that person wins the lottery (the kinder, gentler, "gets hit by a bus"). It can be difficult enough when people leave a company, but it becomes easier when the records are all stored in a known location. If necessary, you might need to implement some processes. While using a records management application is commonsense, commonsense unfortunately needs some processes around it to point people in the right direction.

You might also need to consider a monitoring process. Monitoring the use of the records management application allows you to ensure that people are using it. Additionally, monitoring usage allows you to verify that people can retrieve the records they need. Especially early after implementation, it is important to ensure the application has been configured correctly so people can find the necessary records. If not, it is important to make corrections early so people don't get frustrated and stop using it. Partnering with your users lets them see that you are there to help them.

Handling records is similar to handling data, which is why I cover this in the data governance section.

Data Governance 2.0, Data Governance 3.0, What?!

At one point, people started talking about "Data Governance 2.0." This was quickly followed by "Data Governance 3.0." There might even have been some other numbers. But what does all that mean and how is it different from, I guess, Data Governance 1.0?

Data governance has been around for years. Like most things, it's expected that it will evolve over time. There really isn't a need to put a stake in the ground. "Before this, it was Data Governance 1.0, and after that, it is Data

Governance 2.0." What is really changing and how is it significant enough that a rebranding is necessary?

I can look back at the beginning of data governance and how it was done. That's not exactly how I do it now. I can take something to a client as a starting point, but it can change based on their culture and their issues. It has to fit for them, and we must be willing to make modifications that work. There are things I've done for a client that I've found to be so successful that I've made it part of what I do with other clients. It's part of the evolution, instead of stopping and saying that I'll now call it 2.0 or 3.0.

I suspect it's largely about marketing. Many people and companies are trying to promote data governance and want to differentiate themselves from others. They hope to show differentiation in the marketplace by rebranding with a number. It gives them something to hype.

It finally hit me one day what bothered me the most about it. Using numbers, including decimals, seems to be something that started with software design. It was a way for them to put out a new release and keep track of which version customers were using in case of an issue they needed to research. At any point in time, different customers were using different versions of the software. From a software perspective, it made sense and it's been very helpful. But data governance isn't software.

Data governance needs people, process, and technology. Any software you use can have a release numbering system, but data governance doesn't need it. I don't change one day and start calling myself Merrill 2.0. If someone in the data governance organization moves on and gets replaced, we don't start calling it Data Governance 2.0. We just move on with the new people. If we change a definition or a set of code values, it's helpful to use dates to keep track of when the change happened to the data, but using a numbering system isn't helpful. I think this comes to one of the more confusing aspects people have with data governance. It's not a technology. It's not about buying a software product, installing it, and walking away. Without the people following the right processes, you're dead in the water. If we can leave a software numbering system out of data governance, which is fundamentally a business construct, we're helping the data industry.

When people are trying to learn new concepts, we need to go out of our way to avoid anything confusing.

Data in Real Life—The Meaning of Owners

I was helping a company set up data governance. We had worked through how their organization should be structured and who should be involved. We thought it might help to name these groupings of people. They were really struggling to find appropriate names. I gave them some suggestions based on how other companies had named their groupings. In particular, a lot of people at the time seemed to use "business data owners." I told them that while they didn't have to use that, that particular group made up the owners and shouldn't be confused with the other group, which were more like the stewards, or people who applied the rules coming from the owners.

After a couple of weeks, they came back to me with the names they wanted to use for their groupings. While they liked "owner" and "steward," they had them reversed. They wanted to use "owner" to describe what were "stewards" and vice versa. After some discussion, they were able to explain their reasoning. From their perspective, the stewards were hands on with the data and "owned" the relationship with the data. I understood their point and why there was the confusion. We were eventually able to agree on names that worked for the company.

Since that experience, I rarely use the terms "owner" and "steward." If a company really insists on them, I will use them, but they have to be very clear about what the words mean to them.

Data in Real Life—Everybody Wants to Rule the World

A company grew through acquisition. They had multiple brands, but each operated individually. However, they still had to produce company-wide reports and had difficulty consolidating that data across brands.

One brand decided to take the lead in improving its data situation. As noble as that decision was, it presented problems. Other companies have tried this approach before and it's hard to execute.

When one brand takes the lead, the other brands might become concerned about fair treatment and do not recognize their peers as leaders they should follow. When it's not a corporate approach, it can be hard to get access to the corporate individuals needed as the decision makers.

It can sometimes be better to keep trying to sell the idea at the corporate level to have the most buy-in for success. Be clear in your story and explain why you're currently not successful. In many cases, the people using the company-wide reports don't recognize a problem because you worked too hard on reconciling data, but that hard work was in the background.

Four

Data Architecture

A data architecture explains the context of how a company stores, integrates, and uses data. A data architecture diagram illustrates how the data flows through the applications. Without a clearly thought-out architecture, people often build data silos–isolated standalone databases. That means that they need data and create what they want for that immediate need. Later, they have another need and build that, which might overlap with the other silo, but they find it quicker to build from scratch. Meanwhile, someone in another department needs data and builds something without talking to anyone else and realizing that someone else already created what they need. This chaotic environment continues where you have lots of duplication and lots of lost time creating things you don't need or looking for things you can't find.

A well-designed architecture often includes multiple designs to solve different purposes. For instance, a relational design is critical to understanding the relationships that exist between the data. This design allows you to think thoughtfully about how the business interacts with the data and what it needs to do its job now and in the future. Other designs, such as used in a data warehouse, will aid in reporting but are not a replacement for the relational design. They work together, and each solves a specific purpose.

Many people think of data architecture as technical, which can look that way, but it must be created in collaboration with the business. The business knows the data it uses and the business rules to follow, although not necessarily using that terminology. You need to translate this into a technical design. However, the business might not clearly explain the rules, or the technical team might not understand them correctly. By working together, they can take responsibility for creating the right design for the business. You can't approach it in a technical manner and jump straight to the technical implementation.

> *By ignoring the business, you'll design something that will constantly be changing because you didn't meet the needs of the business.*

If you've already built your data governance organization, you've identified the people across the company who need to be involved in the data architecture. You'll get the complete input you need to develop the data architecture right the first time. Even just having other eyes validate what you've developed helps. We often don't recognize differences from other countries and cultures in this global world. Addresses might be structured differently than what you're used to. Names could be different, such as not all cultures use last names. Or, where are we going to put Cher or Madonna?

Documented correctly, the data architecture can assist in tracing errors. When you have a problem, it is not always a quick fix. Sometimes, a quick fix will cause long-term pain. You need to trace errors back to the source and fix them there. Was a calculation wrong? If so, fix the calculation. You don't want to find yourself in a place where you have to manually manipulate data on a regular basis because you did not want to make the right fix.

Why Do We Care About Data Lineage?

Data lineage is one of those things that people talk about, think they need it, and then put it at the bottom of the pile when timelines get tight. One of my first projects when I started my career was two people walking up to me with two different reports. Each had been convinced for years that their report was right, but then they discovered one day that they each had a line item that should be the same number and it wasn't. At that point, they didn't know what to believe and their trust in the data was gone. Without any data lineage documented, it was an exercise of picking through the various places the data moved and got transformed to come to the true answer. And then fix it!

I sometimes talk about data lineage as data genealogy. That can make it feel more real. You start with some data, find out the parents, the grandparents, etc. Where did the data come from? Where did it go? How did it get there? Why did it get there? I once worked at a client that was developing its own tool to display data lineage called "Who's You Daddy?" That says it right there. Ultimately, you have to prove the parentage of the data without any question.

> *When you give people reports, they should be able to believe what is on the reports without question.*

They should be able to take the reports and start using them. If you're talking about financial statements, they're even more important. Did you test the report thoroughly? Unfortunately, I've seen a lot of people who test reports superficially and don't really understand how to perform data testing. If you're testing the data, you need to prove that it's coming in correctly, being transformed (if necessary) correctly, being stored correctly, and being displayed correctly on reports. You can't do that without a data lineage document to refer to. That is the map that tells you how to get from point A to point B. If you need to, create a visual showing how the data is moving, even if it needs to be printed out and wrapped around the room. (Yes–I've done that!)

Data lineage can also tell you how to treat the data. If there are regulations around certain data elements, you need to know what rules to apply to the data. I worked at a company where they thought the data came from a certain source that prevented them from sending it out of the country. They assumed where the data came from, but not based on any facts. After investigating the data lineage, we determined that the data didn't originate there and thus wasn't restricted in how they thought it was. It was free to leave the country. They had spent years restricting data that they didn't need to restrict. They could have saved years of pain if someone had documented the data lineage originally.

Documenting data lineage can sound mundane, but it's always interesting to do the research and solve problems. It can be very satisfying when you uncover that issue that finally explains why people are seeing different data than they expect, or you determine that data doesn't come from where you thought it did. However, that comes after the fact. Ideally, documenting your data lineage is something you should do as part of your data architecture development and maintenance because it needs to be kept current if there are any changes. If you take that proactive step, it's much easier than being reactive by picking through program code later to figure out what went wrong. No one wants that job. Do it right the first time, and everyone will be happier, especially those who rely on problem-free data. Besides, if you don't have data lineage, how do you test that the data flows correctly? You don't.

You create data lineage at the time you design your data architecture. That's the easiest place to do it because it's fresh in your memory. Doing it after the fact means finding time to do it when you have other tasks to do. Although it represents the data architecture, you can also consider it metadata, which is why I go into more detail about it in the metadata section of this book. But keep in mind who is capable of documenting a data lineage. You need someone who understands data and how it flows. It is not always the same person who can write data definitions, something else often considered part of data architecture as well as part of metadata.

Data in Real Life—Bird Count

At some point, you'll find duplicate data and need to find a resolution. You need to clearly define the rules you will use to determine what data you should be using.

Something similar exists in bird counts. I've never participated in one, but there are national bird counts throughout the year. People volunteer to count birds. On the one hand, it sounds simple. On the other hand, are you serious? Birds move around. You're counting a moving target. You need to organize your volunteers so they're in non-overlapping areas. You have to have some way to estimate the number of birds that leave one area and move into another area, thereby possibly getting counted twice. Architecting that solution is critical and impacts the value of your results.

> *A lot of birds look similar. That doesn't mean they're identical. That's part of the challenge.*

Five

Master Data Management

Master data management, as far as I can recall, was a term created by tool vendors. That's not necessarily bad, but let's dissect it. We've got "master data" in the name. We've got "data management" in the name. We don't have "master data data management" because that would probably be awkward and get caught in a Microsoft Word grammar check, but you get the idea. When we talk about MDM, we're talking about the management of master data. We need to manage it, so that's good. However, we can't forget that not all data is master data, and we must also manage that data. MDM is really just managing a subset of your data.

Some people would argue that. Master data is "special." It's important. It's the most important data we have. Ok, but you still have to follow all your data management principles. You need to govern that master data. You need

101

to have metadata on that master data. That master data better be of high quality. There might be data privacy issues concerning the master data. As you see, we're covering all the same topics with master data as we would with non-master data.

Data management is more of an inclusive approach to managing all data, not just master data. Where the MDM tools come in is that they help you better resolve the duplication you often see in master data. They also help you implement your master data rules, which are often needed because master data has a habit of existing in multiple places. If your customer data currently exists in five applications because you bought the best application for each of the five departments, you can probably say with certainty that the data doesn't always match. Maybe the customer address differs because a customer updated it with sales, but sales didn't tell anyone else. If you're using an MDM tool, it can help you keep track of the real customer address.

I know people who have debated violently whether something is master data or not. In a way, I don't care. It's data used by the business and we need to manage it. Spending too much time debating whether it belongs in one place or another isn't helping the fact that, in the meantime, you're not managing it and it's probably wrong.

Just because it's called master data doesn't mean you've mastered it. The wording difference between an adjective and a verb is subtle, but the impact is great.

MDM—In the Beginning

Before there were MDM tools, there was … data architecture. That's right. Before MDM tools, we just designed the data architecture correctly. Now that we have MDM tools, we can probably perform MDM tasks more completely and efficiently. They're probably quicker too, although I've been through some really long MDM tool implementations. (However, I suspect the vendor actually sold us "vaporware" and they built the tool after I kept asking them very specific questions.)

MDM is all about rules. Despite what some people may think, MDM is not about installing a magical tool that fixes all your data problems. The tool can only do what you tell it to do. You have to define the rules. You have to configure the tool to use those rules. You have to test that tool like crazy to make sure that it performs as intended. Only then can you implement the tool into production. If you think about MDM before MDM tools, it was still about the rules. You still had to define the rules. You still had to have someone code the rules. You still had to test it. Some people might refer to it as more of a "brute force" approach, but it got the job done. This is why those of us who truly understand MDM focus on the rules instead of the tool.

> *If you don't get the rules right, there's no hope for the tool. The tool needs those rules to be effective.*

Think of a situation like a merger or acquisition. Maybe you weren't mastering your data and had customer data in five different databases. Then the merger happens, but they also had customer data in five different databases. Unless you master your customer data, you now have customer data in ten different databases. It's highly unlikely that data will be identical. You had a problem before the merger, but now your problem is so much worse. You can't work with the customer with any level of confidence because you don't know which of the ten versions of customer data is accurate. A merger or acquisition can be great for your business, but don't forget your data.

We need to know how we will handle duplicates, or maybe we need to call them similars. When we have duplicate data, it's probably ok when they truly are the same. Is there harm if they're in multiple places but always identical? You need to do the work to keep them in sync though. The problem comes when they're not the same. You've got customer address in multiple places and it's not the same address, so you don't know which one is right. They may look similar, but they're not identical. That's the challenge your rules need to address.

MDM—Bringing on the Magic

We know that MDM means Master Data Management. In a creative fit, I offered up "Make Data Magical." And it caught on! We enter an MDM project because of a business need. There have probably been issues with bad data and suspicious reports. We can be transformative when we can work through those issues and devise a rule-based solution that reduces the need to manipulate bad data into good (or semi-good).

We can change the business into thinking about what the data tells them rather than griping over how bad the data is.

MDM has a bit of a publicity problem. Many people have heard the buzzword and think they need it. The problem comes when they find out there's a cost associated with it, and they have to determine if they can afford it. If you're making business decisions on bad data though, how can you not afford it? Since MDM is being built behind the scenes for most people, they don't really understand the impact it can have. Maybe we need to bring on the magic, which might help people understand it. Make it real instead of explaining it as a theoretical concept that supports the infrastructure. Explain scenarios through the problems you have today and how much better the scenario will be in the future. You often need to write a business case to get the funding, so make sure people understand the reason for MDM–the need for the magic.

People are often asked to quantify the value of MDM. This can be a difficult task, but remember that there are tangibles and intangibles. Sometimes, it can be easier to communicate the intangibles, but you do have to be clear in your communications. The difficulty with tangibles is quantifying how much time you spend working around your data problems. You know you have problems, you have hacks to get around the problems, but you get your job done. It might take longer than expected to deliver or take long work hours, but you deliver. You can be so good at your job that the people using the data or seeing the data on reports are unaware of a data problem. You have hidden the data behind the curtain.

Address harmonization–You may need a customer master solution if you've got multiple customer addresses and can't figure out which one is right, you're sending product (especially time-sensitive or temperature-sensitive product) to the wrong customer address, you're sending sales reps to the wrong location, etc. If you can resolve these issues, it can feel magical.

Data consolidation–We've seen home makeover shows where someone's closet is transformed magically overnight into an organized thing of beauty. While it doesn't usually happen overnight, organizing your data can have the same effect. Knowing where everything is, you can easily find it when needed. People want to start using data and determining insights from it. People don't want to waste time hunting around for data, asking questions, and either manipulating it or finding a workaround.

Single source of the truth–It's natural to source data from multiple locations, but you need to know the right data. You don't want to waste time hunting for the right data and still not be positive about your answer. Analytics generated from a squishy foundation will yield squishy results. Build an MDM solution based on business rules that build that single source of the truth.

Unified view of data–Having a single view of your data allows you to see its history. In this mobile world, you want to stay in contact with your customers if they move. You want to understand your history with that customer in one location and take that knowledge when the customer relocates. Unifying that data allows people to make decisions more quickly because they don't need to spend time reconciling data before they can use it.

Accurate decisions–Are you unknowingly making poor decisions because you don't understand your data? As much as people grumble, documentation is your friend! People often guess what data means but base that guess on a brief name in a report or an even briefer column name in a database table. There can be plenty of business terms with similar names or names to qualify in a context. For this reason, you need to understand what the data means before using it. With terms defined, business rules documented, and calculations recorded, you can use the data correctly and make accurate decisions.

Better decision making–How many of us have seen technical diagrams showing data going into a box (or worse, a black box) and something coming out the other end? This is true magic. You don't know what happened in that box. To make appropriate decisions or perhaps have confidence in your data in a highly regulated environment, you must understand where it came from and what transformations it underwent. Otherwise, you hope the puff of smoke yielded data you can believe in.

Improved employee experience–Bad data managed by bad data management processes gets propagated throughout the company and potentially worldwide, depending on your company's reach. That expands the impact of the problem. You want people to have the data they need when they need it and not frustrate them by having them find a less reputable source of the data they need.

Improved confidence–Implemented properly, MDM improves confidence in data because you're following official business rules and developing a repeatable and trustworthy solution. You're building a solid foundation of data that people can use appropriately. You want the magic to be in the insights you deliver from good data, not in the unknown actions performed on the data.

It's time to bring magic into your data. Implement MDM and bring the value of good data to your organization. Be transparent and let people know what's happening with the data. There's power in data. Reveal the magic. Make Data Magical!

Governing MDM Programs

A company that chooses to spend money on an MDM program but doesn't implement any data governance solution has only done a disservice to itself. Without data governance, the time and money spent on MDM goes to waste. That doesn't mean you must spend a lot of time and money on a data governance solution. But data governance is definitely a requirement. If we go back to the initial comments about MDM being data management over master data, you need to follow the same data management capabilities you would follow on non-master data.

A retail business with many locations might have problems managing their product data and choose to select product as a master data domain. They spend time analyzing the various products each location sells. They create standards and standardize their products. They convert data. Finally, they declare the implementation of their product master data complete. That clean, standardized data won't last long if they do nothing else. They must have some governance processes to maintain that pristine data.

Data governance goes hand-in-hand with implementing an MDM program. You do yourself a disservice if you don't implement data governance as a component of your MDM program. Some businesses choose to create a data governance organization. The data governance organization should have the necessary people to make decisions on the master data. Some business people see this as a technology issue and assume that the IT department will make these decisions. However, most of the issues that come before a data governance organization are business-related questions. For instance, if someone wants to expand the definition of the product master data domain, the business should look into how that change would affect current and future products. If someone wants to create new valid values for a product type code, the business people should again look at it to make sure that the values are distinct and non-overlapping. It doesn't come from technology.

The ideal mix in a data governance organization combines business and technology staff but heavy on the business. By having both groups working together, you'll be able to find the best solution for the organization. Business people should know more about what is happening in the business now and in the future. However, the technology people will be able to look at a business decision and determine if there are any technical constraints to it and provide timelines on how long it might take to implement if it requires a technical solution. It's business-led but technology-supported.

When changing master data, documentation must be in place. If you have a formal data governance organization, you probably also have a formal process in place for proposing changes, taking proposals to the data governance organization, approving, documenting, and implementing.

It's important to remember that the implementation of MDM is a program, not a project. Once implemented, you don't walk away from it and never look at it again. You need to have the appropriate governance in place to maintain the data as the business evolves and respond to issues that arise.

Data in Real Life—Make Data Magical

I worked with a company that had a tremendous number of master data issues. Specifically, customer data had so many flaws that caused people to waste too many hours trying to figure out what was wrong. Sales reps weren't getting the sales credits they had earned because there were conflicts trying to figure out which customer it was. Customers had multiple addresses and identifying numbers. People thought they were entering the right data, but things were just getting more confused.

After years of problems, the company finally agreed to commit to fixing the problem once and for all. This required implementing a master data solution. A master data vendor was chosen. We went through the usual project hiccups as we designed and tested, but the day finally arrived. We ran it overnight and I arrived in the morning to see what we were dealing with. It worked! Some records errored, but we quickly realized what had happened and were able to fix the problem. After that, it worked so smoothly. I was talking to someone one day about it and coined the phrase "Make Data Magical" for MDM because that's exactly what had happened. Instead of spending days trying to figure out data issues, we essentially resolved them overnight. Ok—not exactly overnight because of the months we spent defining and testing rules, but it was an overnight implementation run. Months later, we would pass each other in the hallway and just shake our heads at how much our lives had changed. Instead of solving data problems every day, we had time to devote to other important tasks.

Data in Real Life—Buying Master Data

I worked at a company that recognized that they had a big problem with customer data. They recognized this as a master data issue, which it was, but they didn't take the right approach to fix it. The IT department advised the business to buy another company's customer master. It was true that they needed a customer master. However, they needed their own customer master, not someone else's.

I'm not sure how this happened. I'm assuming that people probably heard the term "master data" and felt that would solve the problem, but they didn't take the time to actually understand what the concept meant. When they first talked to me, they threw out lots of terms that made me realize that they knew terms, but didn't know how they all fit together. It took some time to unravel what happened, but I finally realized they bought a vendor's customer master. Why the vendor even sold it is questionable, but I guess some people do strange things to make money. It might have been a good purchase for certain situations, but not what this company did with it. They ultimately wound up in a worse situation than what they started with. They had another vendor's customer master, which still didn't match their own transactional data, so they wasted time trying to match them up. It wasn't an easy discussion to get them to realize that this wasn't a survivable solution and that they would eventually have to build their own customer master.

Data in Real Life—What is the Customer Address?

A company had a product recall. They were required to mail a notice to all their customers, notifying them not to use the product. Unfortunately, they hadn't mastered their customer data. They had a tremendous number of recall notices returned to them due to either an undeliverable address or the customer no longer being at that address. Depending on the product, this can be very serious. For instance, it becomes extremely serious if customers shouldn't take a recalled medication.

In this case, the problem was so significant that the company failed an audit, was imposed a fine, and was ordered to create a customer master.

Six

Data Modeling

A data model depicts how a company uses information. You can think of it as a pictorial representation, but it's more than just a pretty picture. You'll have a picture with boxes, lines, and symbols, but that's just the picture portion of the data model. You also have metadata that goes along with it. In fact, most data model tools have functionality to store the metadata as well. Putting your metadata there is convenient because it's tied exactly to the picture and you can easily see if you're missing anything, such as forgetting to enter some definitions. The downside is that not everyone can access the tool, so they can't see the metadata unless you export everything for them. If you choose to put your metadata elsewhere, you will have to perform regular validation to make sure that the picture is consistent with the metadata. It is too easy to add something to the picture and forget to add it to the metadata.

Having the definitions with your data model gives it context so people can understand the diagram. People unfamiliar with data models need those definitions. However, even the creator of the data models might forget what things mean over time. Data models can get very extensive and there can be nuances between attributes, so the definitions give you the clarity you need.

Some people leave out the definitions, thinking that it takes too much time or that they've spent so much time on the diagram that they know exactly what it means. However, it might not be as clear as you think it is. Something that sounds simple, like "customer," needs a definition so you know what a customer means to this company. Is it just current customers? (How do you define "current"?) Is it historic customers? Is it prospects? Sometimes you can further examine the diagram to get the answers, but you don't want to examine the diagram every time to answer a simple question.

What I want to see with a data model are entity definitions, attribute definitions, code values, and sometimes even relationship definitions if they're not clear. Code values are essential in knowing how the data model works. For instance, you need to understand the values for things like "customer type" or "product type." Those classifications can lead you elsewhere in the model because some attributes only apply to certain classifications.

If you create a proper data model, you have definitions, data types, data lengths, code values, etc. You have all the things that often later get called metadata. Save yourself from a big metadata project in the future by creating everything with the data model so it's complete and cohesive.

Sometimes, your data model contains some complex concepts. In this case, you should take the time to prepare a document that explains those concepts in easy-to-understand language. I prefer to create a document that includes images of those hard-to-understand concepts. The images might contain a few entities along with their attributes, relationships, and a textual explanation. Then, I'll have another version of that image annotated with sample data so the reader can better understand the complex concepts surrounding that part of the data model.

There are different types of data models, so know what you need.

Consider conceptual, logical, and physical. Consider relational and dimensional. Consider if you're creating a really large data model that you have to print on a plotter (or tape together), or my preferred method, dividing your data model into manageable subject areas. If you do use subject areas, make sure you clearly show all linkages between subject areas. Realize that this is not a standalone activity. A data modeler will have to work with the business. If you've established your data governance organization, you know who you're working with and who approves the design before it goes into production.

Creating and maintaining data models needs to follow a good methodology. It's important to remember the maintenance part. The company will likely evolve and you will need to change the data model. Everything will need to be approved and documented before it goes into production.

Logical Relational Data Modeling—Where It All Started

I believe in a good logical data model. Specifically, relational. Some people try to start with dimensional modeling, but they completely miss the value that comes from a relational model. A logical relational data model will show the relationships between data. It's where you'll see what data the business needs and how they use it. It will allow you to truly understand the data. That relational model is critical.

> *Don't try to jump a step by starting with a dimensional model, which is helpful for reporting but often contains data redundancies. Skipping the relational model will add too much complexity to reporting.*

I learned logical modeling at school where they taught a tool-agnostic approach. There are tool vendors who will teach you, but then you get the version of how to do it in their tool instead of a more "pure" version. You might miss some modeling concepts because that vendor does not support them. You get the quick-and-dirty of using the tool instead of what a data model means and how to create it. You might know how to use the tool, but do you understand what to put in it?

When you start with a data model, you can easily fit it into your data management program. Deciding what goes into the model and how the data is related means working with the business people you've identified in your data governance organization. Creating that model with its definitions and code values means you get metadata to validate through your data governance organization. You are seeing how your data management program is beneficial to the company.

While I might appear biased since I started my career in relational modeling, I think you learn so much from it. You have the overall picture of what your data infrastructure looks like, you see how data is related to other data, you have definitions, you have data lineage, and you've been communicating with business people. You work with DBAs to get a logical model converted to a physical model and implemented. You are involved with any production problems because an error in the design or implementation could cause them.

I've often struggled to respond when people ask me how to get started in a career in data management. It's hard to see something beyond my experience. It doesn't come from a tool vendor. That gives you a skewed view of how the tool looks at the world. Get yourself into a relational data modeling class that's tool-agnostic.

Data in Real Life—One or Two Households?

Many companies use the concept of householding to identify their customers who live together. It can be helpful to know how to market to the household, but also make sure you recognize each household member as a separate individual. There might also be separate ways to market to each customer.

A mother and daughter had separate accounts at the same bank. The mother added the daughter to her account for possible emergency situations.

The daughter used an ATM to withdraw some cash from her bank account and was surprised at the bank balance. The bank had made a mistake and linked the daughter's ATM card to the mother's bank account.

Unless there was an emergency, the daughter wanted to access her own account. She didn't need to access her mother's account. She never authorized the bank to link her ATM card to her mother's account.

The householding concept has been around for decades, and you can handle it through a proper data design. This bank had all the data but shuffled it up a bit. They lost track of who each of their customers was and lost how to properly market to each customer.

Data in Real Life—A Place for All the Data

While registering on a website, I saw that the field for last name said "Last Name (generally includes suffix: e.g., JR, SR, III)." "Generally" is not really a good idea. It either is or it isn't.

From a data perspective, every field should be stored uniquely. There should be a last name field and a suffix field. If you want to merge them for customer data entry purposes, understand what you're doing and the implications.

Will Bob Smith Jr know to enter it all now or think there will be a field later for Jr? Will you eventually be able to distinguish between Bob Smith and Bob Smith Jr? And what about Bob Smith and Dr Bob Smith? There was no prefix field, or even a "generally" comment. Not everyone has a prefix, but when they do, you have to know where you're storing it. If you have a customer list, will the list be in order by first name or prefix? It can make working with data difficult when fields aren't being used uniquely.

Seven

Data Lakes

As data has evolved, someone came up with the term "data lake." Later, someone came up with the term "data lakehouse." Are these real? You can definitely think of differences related to what is stored in them and how they're accessed, but do you need to make the distinction? Is it just about marketing? Can we just call them all databases?

Governing Data Lakes

Some people wonder how to govern a data lake. What is different about governing a data lake than any other database? I contend that it is essentially the same. You still need all the same components of governance. The only difference is what you're governing.

I've developed many data governance organizations. They all have some of the same components—an organization of people performing various roles, processes, policies, templates, charter, decision-making, communications, etc. What's always different is what the organization chooses to govern. What is sometimes related is the organization's level of maturity in its data management, and its business problems. For that reason, I think of governing a data lake as fitting easily into the same rules of governing anything else. A data lake is just a newer buzzword, and there's always a new buzzword.

Are the people wanting a data lake the same people who ignore data governance and gave us the term "data swamp"? Whether we're talking about a data lake or not, what we want to avoid is the swamp—the place where data gets lost in the murky depths and dies. You're pretty sure it's there; you just can't find it.

When creating a data lake, starting with data governance is essential. Data governance becomes more difficult to implement after creating the data lake because that's when you're playing catch up and going on an archaeological dig to figure out what they put in the data lake. Whether a data lake or an "ordinary" database, you still need to know what's in it, what it means, and how to use it properly. You're probably building the data lake to make it more convenient and efficient for the data scientists to do their work. They can be very good at analysis, but if they don't have good data at the start, the insights they generate will lack value or be of questionable value. Good data governance positions them for success. In fact, this can be the scariest part of creating a data lake. People who think a

DATA LAKES • 123

data lake allows them to avoid data governance will probably generate a mess.

One of the differences with a data lake is that you might use it more for analysis than your operational database. You might be "playing" with the data to see how bringing together different data sets tells a different story than you can see operationally. If so, you'll want to capture metadata around your analytics so you can transfer something trustworthy to production. What calculations are used? Do all decision makers agree on the calculations? Where does the data being used come from? Is the source data trustworthy? You'll want to have your analytics clearly defined if you plan to promote some of them into your operational environment. You don't want to impede the process of the data scientists, but you do need to ensure that the analytics used in production are defined, trustworthy, repeatable, consistent, and defendable.

Technologies evolve. Buzzwords come and go. Just don't get mesmerized by the latest bright shiny object and forget about the good discipline of data governance.

Data in Real Life—What's in My Data Lake?

A company jumped on the data lake bandwagon. They thought it would be an exciting opportunity to have their data scientists have access to all their raw data and perhaps come up with some interesting insights that they weren't able to do with the regular databases that were in production. Everything went into the data lake–all data from production databases, original source data, external vendor data, manipulations from various spreadsheets, etc. All the data they thought they might need or want went into the data lake.

Since they approached their data lake like their kitchen junk drawer, everything went into it and people didn't really know what was in there. There might be multiple versions of customer addresses because they came from different places. If someone tried to do analysis based on customer address, they would have to choose the right one to get the right results. Without any documentation of what was in the data lake, they had a quagmire they could not decipher.

How do you fix that? You're really in a position where you have to start from scratch, but be more careful the next time. Track what goes into the data lake. Document everything. It will make analysis a lot easier.

Eight

Metadata

M etadata is "data about data," but does that help people understand it? Metadata is "data about data" because metadata can actually be many things, so the definition must remain generic. It often depends on the context in which you use the term metadata, leading people to talk about it as "data about data in context." The problem with metadata is that it can be anything. I've often found that examples help people understand it better than just saying "data about data."

Metadata helps people understand the data so they use it properly. If there are problems understanding what the data means, it's generally the company's own fault. Metadata is also something that you shouldn't wait on. If you create it while doing another task, it can be easier for people to remember rather than waiting months (or years!) before undertaking it. Definitions are a great example of metadata, but if people skip them thinking the definition is obvious, they'll often be surprised. Another example is data lineage, which was originally created alongside a data model. You needed the data lineage to test that your design was correct. Unfortunately, as people have tried to jump over data modeling, they've also jumped over data lineage. As people come back to realizing they need data lineage, it often gets classified under metadata.

> *As long as you have the right people creating it, the right people validating it, and you do it before you need it, I don't get too concerned about where it sits. I care that it gets done because it serves a purpose.*

I've only recently started hearing non-data people embrace the term. Unfortunately, it's usually in the context of metadata about photos or documents during a forensics investigation. So, it's not in a good situation, but people are starting to hear and understand the term.

When you have a data model, metadata is the data that describes other data on that data model. In other words, metadata can be the textual description of an entity. It can also be the valid values of an attribute. It can also be the length of a database column. The metadata gives context to the data. Some specific examples follow.

- If you have an entity called address, it might have attributes of street address, city, and state. Although these are often referred to as attributes, they're also metadata for that entity. It depends on how you use the term metadata.

- The address entity might have the definition, "The specific site where the client is located." This definition is metadata for the entity.

- Within the address entity, the state attribute might have the definition, "The code representing the state within the United States where the client is located." This definition is metadata for the attribute.

- For the attribute state, it's defined as being of character value of length 2 and mandatory. Character, 2, and mandatory are all metadata for the attribute.

- The attribute state might also have a set of valid values consisting of "NY," "FL," etc. These values are metadata for the attribute.

Some people distinguish between "business metadata" and "technical metadata." I will do that if people want it, but I generally don't bother. It's metadata and we need it all. I don't think the debate of whether it's classified in the right group is furthering the process of getting it done, and that debate can last a long time and get heated without generating any metadata.

Once we agree on the definition of metadata, we can talk about maintaining this metadata. It can change over time, so it is important to monitor and update it if necessary. For instance, a business can grow over time. Maybe a new product will require a new value for product type code. Some people talk about "metadata management," although that probably comes more from implementing a metadata tool in isolation of data management.

If you're doing data management right, metadata fits right into it as what you manage. You need the right governance in place to make decisions with the right people. You need to know where the most up-to-date metadata is. Like other data, you need a single version of the truth for your metadata. You need a change process that identifies who has the authority to change the metadata and who needs to be notified of proposed changes. You need to consider tracking historical versions of the metadata since that could impact your referential integrity. In addition, you will need to define how people will access the metadata and where it will reside. You can create a data model with the entities and attributes in your metadata strategy. Your data model will include definitions and valid values. In effect, you've created metadata about your metadata and you've come full circle.

Dictionaries

What's in a dictionary? That might sound like a strange question, but I've seen both good and bad dictionaries. There was a time when we just created dictionaries in data modeling tools, so the dictionary contained whatever the tool said it would. Usually, this means a name and definition. If you used the tool right, you could produce additional reports showing where the entity was used, and then after you produced the physical model, you could get a report on database classifications (e.g., data type, length).

As we continued to work with data, we quickly realized a name and definition weren't enough. We needed to know additional features of the data (e.g., how it is used, security restrictions on the data, privacy restrictions on the data, data lineage, etc.).

We can capture this information in spreadsheets, in-house tools, or off-the-shelf tools. Now, you're truly building metadata.

Companies often have multiple vendor applications. Ideally, the vendor has a dictionary that comes with it. If you have ten applications and ten dictionaries, chances are high that some (ok, all) of those definitions will be different. You then have to decide what you're going to do next. Do you create a company dictionary that holds everything so you can see the variability? Do you create a company dictionary that only contains the overall company version of the definition? Do you tell people not to look at the vendor dictionaries? Your infrastructure can be complicated, so you need to be clear with people.

You can also extend your data dictionary/metadata tool to include analytics. You've taken the time to figure out what analytics you need, so make sure you use them successfully. Multiple people might be developing similar analytics, so you want to consolidate your efforts and use the same terminology and calculations.

You want a definition for your analytics. How do you use analytics? Where are they used? What calculations are involved? Presumably, you want to be able to repeat the calculations, so you better document well so you remember how to do that. Does this sound familiar? I've just listed things we have in the dictionary.

Buying Metadata

I've seen companies try to buy metadata, specifically definitions. They know they need it, they know it will take more time to create than they want, they think they can just take a shortcut, and they buy metadata from a vendor. Just because a vendor describes something one way doesn't mean you do as well. Your company might work differently, and the definitions might differ for you.

Most companies work with numerous vendors and each vendor can define terms differently. That complicates how those tools interact with each other. Just because multiple tools use the same name does not mean they're defining it and using it the same way. If you purchased a tool, it should come with metadata. Check your contract so they don't try to ask you to pay more for it. Part of the acquisition process should include exactly what you're getting with the tool.

Don't think of definitions as a check-the-box activity you just want to get over with. You don't just buy them all and declare success. Write the right definitions for you. When I write definitions, I look at what business people in each department say, how IT implemented it, what the industry says, what the dictionary says, etc. Take that input and get your definition written, revised, and approved through the data governance organization. Then, if your applications are not using the data correctly, fix them.

Data in Real Life—Who Works for Us?

A CEO wanted to send all employees a new product they were about to release. He thought it was a simple request. But his request threw the department heads into a tailspin.

Who were the employees? The problem is that each department defined employee differently. They had full-time and part-time employees. They were also in a business that had seasonal employees. They had some recent acquisitions that weren't entirely complete and integrated yet. They had lengthy meetings trying to define who their employees were.

The problem they were having is that they knew what employee meant within each department. At the higher company level, they just couldn't agree. Meetings over months finally created a solution. By that time, the product was already on the market, so the CEO missed the goal of getting it to employees before the release date.

It is likely this was a problem before this request. The company must have had consolidated reports that developers struggled to create because they had to reconcile employee. What they should have done was create the definitions before there was a crisis. There will always be a crisis after implementation.

Data in Real Life—We Don't Have That Problem. We Have That Documented.

I was interviewing someone at a company. During a discussion on metadata, I used an example from another company I had talked to where people sometimes have different definitions for the same term. She listened to and understood the example, but told me they didn't have that problem. In fact, she stated that the particular term I mentioned was defined in high-level company documentation, so they couldn't misuse it. They knew exactly what it meant.

The truth is that I had already interviewed some other people at the company and knew that they did have this problem with that exact term. They had numerous siloed applications and some applications defined the term differently.

Just because a term is documented doesn't mean people use it that way. Unless you're enforcing the definitions, there's a chance that people aren't using them properly. In this case, the company had not yet established data management. There was no responsibility for creating definitions or monitoring definitions. People stumbled across the problem when they were trying to consolidate data from other departments and discovered inconsistencies in the data.

Nine

Data Quality

Data quality is more than just having good data. What really is "good"? Within the same company, one person's good is someone else's bad. You need to understand what quality means to you to have the confidence you need to use the data appropriately.

Confidence in the data extends beyond the company's walls. If you have data quality issues, it probably isn't contained internally. If your customers see data quality issues, they can quickly lose confidence in you. You want to quickly find and address problems before hearing customer complaints. If you do find problems, make sure you communicate them. It's better to be up front about data quality than try to mask the problem and be exposed later. Be proactive, not reactive.

If you find a data quality problem, it's important to fix it at the source of the problem—the root cause.

You will always be fixing the same data over and over again if you see bad data on a report and just tweak the report to alter the data, or you see bad data on a screen displayed to a customer and just alter the data in the report database. Also, your little tweak might change the data that other people are using for other purposes, making their reports wrong. There could even be legal implications to manipulating data. What you want to do is fix the data once and for all. That might mean tracking the problem back to a bad calculation and fixing the program code. It might mean tracking the problem back to an employee entering data incorrectly, which should be an easy fix to instruct the employee. You might also track the problem back to a file received from a vendor. In this case, you can talk to the vendor to resolve the data issue, which could be a contract issue.

Think about it in terms of solving or treating a problem. In medicine, there are some problems that we can't solve right now, but we can treat them. The treatment may be lengthy, even life-long. It may be painful. But lots of problems have cures that prevent painful treatments. Don't just treat your data! If you do, you often create a life-long process of changing data. If you can fix the root cause, you've solved the problem by finding the cure. The alternative is changing the data whenever it comes in wrong. If it comes in wrong weekly from a vendor feed, you've created a weekly operational process for yourself.

Data Quality—More Than Just Following Your Gut

Do you follow a disciplined approach with data quality or just poke around the database to see if the data looks "right"? Can you prove you have high-quality data or does your gut tell you it is so? To do data quality right, you have to follow a disciplined approach. Follow business and technical rules to produce reports that prove data quality.

The first premise behind data quality is to not allow bad data into the database in the first place.

If you have an interface where people enter data, use strict controls so people can't enter bad data. If you're loading a data set, use strict controls to check for bad data and don't bring it in. That sounds simplistic, but you must spend time on the rules identifying the data as "bad." Also, there might be times when you decide that some bad data is acceptable to bring in. For instance, if you're loading a large data set, you might decide to accept some problematic data so that you don't lose the entire data set or don't have a delay in getting the data loaded. If there's a user interface, you might want your customers to continue using it even though they're giving you some bad data. But, it's important to remember that if you have made some concessions and decided to bring in bad data, you must fix it after the fact. You might run some regular health checks against the database and then go through an exercise to fix the source of the problem to get good data.

Like everything else with data, you need to think of the three things that act on data—people, process, and technology. You need the right people to define the data quality rules because data quality means different things to different people. You also need the right people monitoring those rules and maybe creating data quality reports. There will likely be a remediation step because the data probably isn't perfect. There are data quality tools that can help, but they're not miracle workers. They're as good as the data quality rules you ask them to check for, and those rules come from the people.

When you're defining good data, how do you define "good"? There's the rub! Good is not what feels right and what allows you to sleep at night. Good has all sorts of dimensions, and many people use the same or similar dimensions. Who knew there were so many ways to define what "good" means? When working on data quality, think about dimensions like accuracy, completeness, conformity, consistency, integrity, timeliness, and uniqueness. While you don't necessarily need everything on day one, start with known problems and expand from there.

Another issue with data quality comes down to the old business versus technology debate. Who defines what is good quality? The business might ask the technology team to implement a data quality tool, but they can't stop there. They need to take responsibility for the business rules and define what "good" means to them. Left to their own devices, the technology team can easily come up with some of the standard things that lots of people have wrong with their databases–inconsistent date formats, jumbled name columns, non-standardized addresses, etc. Those are great things to check for, but your technology team might not know all the things that are important to the business–a missing address might be fine in some cases but not in others, some columns that are missing might prevent the business from working with a customer, etc. Sometimes, the technical desire to prevent a job from failing might cause a bad decision to be made, such as selecting a default value for a column that the business would have selected differently. These nuances of the data need to be communicated and implemented.

Although the data quality rules must come from the business, they probably don't realize they know them. They probably won't say, "We have a data quality problem." They will say, "This number's wrong." "These numbers should match." "I don't trust this number." "I don't know where this number came from." "Can I sign off on this report and submit it?" You have to realize that they're questioning the underlying data and dig into where those questions come from. That will get you to the rules.

Most of the time, we don't have the luxury of starting fresh with an empty database. We embark on a data quality program on an existing database or move data from a legacy database to a shiny new one. Either way, we have to deal with the data that currently exists. I call it an archaeological dig to figure out what's in there and then what you will do with it. What can you fix? What needs to stay because of referential integrity? We're always trying to fix what we can.

Remember that this is a "program." This is not a one-time activity. If you just embark on data quality as a clean-up activity and then walk away, all you've done is fix the data once and it will be bad again tomorrow or even later today. You need to actively monitor the quality of your data on a regular basis.

However you decide to approach a data quality program, remember to take a structured approach.

If you just follow your gut, you're going to get somewhere, but you're probably going to create a hodgepodge with pockets of good data and pockets of bad. In the end, that doesn't build the level of trust in the data you need.

It Doesn't Stop at a Dashboard

When a company realizes that it has data quality problems, it might create a dashboard or buy a data quality tool that has a dashboard. This allows them to easily see what the problems are and monitor progress in improving data quality. However, it's important to understand what you get out of dashboards along with their limitations.

Understand your data quality problems

If you have a dashboard, what data quality problems does it display? Are they superficial (e.g., a US address must have a ZIP Code) or more business-oriented (e.g., we need an email address or a phone number to reach the customer)? Determining your rules should be more than just thinking about data quality off the top of your head. Follow a disciplined approach of examining data quality dimensions: accuracy, completeness, conformity, consistency, integrity, timeliness, and uniqueness.

Who created the business rules represented through the dashboard? If they were created by the data quality tool vendor, or even by your own IT department, they might likely be more superficial. A tool vendor will use rules that are generic-enough to work for all their clients. You just have to make sure you think of them as a starting point only. You need those data quality rules, but you also need the business rules. The business has to be involved in their creation. Recognize that the business owns the rules, but IT owns the implementation of the rules.

You're being shortsighted if you just look at the current data to determine the data quality rules. Looking at the current data tells you what your data currently looks like. It's not necessarily right. It's just what's in the database now. More than likely, looking at the current data tells you what some of the problems are and is the starting point for a subset of data quality rules. Also, look at what the industry says. That might show places where the data in the database doesn't match what's typical in the industry. Most important though, talk to people. People who have been living with this data often know what some of the problems are and what the data quality rules should be to prevent the problems they're seeing.

Understanding the dashboard

What is really on the dashboard? Many dashboards use a graph or speedometer to pictorially show you how good your data is. These can be helpful to give you a quick visual, but you also need to understand what it truly means. If your dashboard says that your customer data is 90% good, do you celebrate that or worry about the 10%? Does the 90%

contain all the data quality checks you need? Is the 90% an average, so some checks are actually higher and some are lower? You need to understand what that number means. While it's helpful to quantify data quality, you must remember that anything less than 100% means you have a data quality problem. There is very real data behind those numbers and very real people trying to use that data.

Resolve data quality problems

If your dashboard shows that your data quality is less than 100%, then you have problems to fix. While you won't necessarily solve everything or solve it immediately, you should report it to your users so they understand the risk if they have to use that data. A good dashboard will also have a component that identifies those problems. That allows you to investigate the error and solve it. Take the philosophy of solving the problem at the source. If you don't, it means that you will constantly have a data quality problem. If an employee is entering data incorrectly, someone needs to tell the employee so it won't happen again. If a vendor sends data incorrectly, someone needs to tell the vendor so it won't happen again. It might even be part of the vendor contract to supply data of a certain quality. Data quality should not be about putting people in roles where they spend their days fixing the same data quality problem over and over again. That's not satisfying for anyone, and it's completely unnecessary if you fix the problem at the source.

Communicate

So, you have a dashboard, but do people know about it? Too often, the dashboard is produced as a means to an end, but remember what the content of that dashboard means. If the data quality is less than 100%, people need to know about it.

People need to know what risk they're taking when they use the data and the impact it could have on their work.

How you communicate it is important. Just sending the dashboard to people might not help because people unfamiliar with the dashboard might find it confusing. You might have to clearly explain to people what it means to them. To some people, the data might not be sufficient for them to do their work. To others, they might be using the portion of the data that's 100% good, so they can proceed without any issues. The data is good enough to some because their work doesn't need perfection.

An example

Think about a simple example of addresses. Does your dashboard say your addresses are 100% good because every column is populated? That might not be the best way to define 100%. All too often, people just want to move on to the next screen, so they'll take shortcuts to enter data just to move along. That might be throwing "11111" into a ZIP Code field just because the application says it's required.

Maybe the dashboard says your addresses are 90% good. An address has multiple components of street address, city, state, and ZIP Code, so is defining data quality on a full address appropriate? If you're dealing with multiple countries, you also need a country component and probably have to consider postal code instead of ZIP Code. If all you care about is ZIP Code, you don't care if the other components are good or bad. However, you don't want to be surprised by bad ZIP Codes because the other address components were good and skewed the data quality up to 90%.

If your dashboard tells you that your addresses are 90% good, is 90% good enough? Think about what you're doing with the data. If you're mailing marketing material, maybe it's fine that 10% of mail could be returned. Is it a cost of doing business, as opposed to the cost of fixing the 10%? If you're mailing information on a data breach instead of a marketing campaign, would your answer be different about whether or not 90% is good enough? Perhaps you're doing analytics and your algorithm requires ZIP Code for the location. In that case, you might not care that someone messed up the rest of the address as long as they got the ZIP Code correct. If they got the ZIP Code wrong though, such as defaulting it to "11111" if they didn't know the real ZIP Code, your analytics are going to be impacted. Suddenly, a lot of people are living in a potential fictitious ZIP Code.

In summary

Dashboards can be really helpful in giving you a quick visual of the quality of the data. Don't leave it at looking at a dashboard. That dashboard can tell you that there are very real data issues that need to be fixed. And if they aren't fixed, those data issues can cause very real business problems.

Cleaning, Cleansing, Fixing, Solving

I cringe a little when people talk about cleaning or cleansing data. The truth is, cleaning data does have a place. That place just usually isn't everyday operations, which is generally when people try using the term. If you plan to convert data from one database to another and then decommission the old database, you often have a data cleaning step in your project plan. You're going to be putting all your data into a shiny new database. Who wouldn't want to take that opportunity to put good data into that database?

In that scenario, you take the opportunity to clean the data before moving it into the new database. That cleaning effort involves things like finding missing values. Maybe your new database has required columns that were optional in the old database. In that case, you need to figure out what the values need to be. You might also consider default values, but consider if that makes sense. I've seen my share of database columns with the value of something like "converted." They're essentially saying it's a required column and the data person made me do it. If you need that column for analytics, "converted" isn't going to cut it.

I've seen people try to fix the data. That might be typing over the value if they have access to the database or it could mean typing over the value in an Excel spreadsheet before creating a report. Unless you're really good at documenting, what you've done is you've lost all tracking. If someone questions a value, you don't have proof of what was done. You've manipulated the data to what you think it should be, but maybe you're wrong. If you find out you're wrong and try returning to the original value, you might have difficulty finding it. Plus, so much data is related to other data, so changing one value probably meant others needed to change that you didn't know about. You've probably created a lot of inconsistencies, which is even worse if there's an audit.

I've known companies that have brought in consultants to fix the data. They seem to do a great job. They leave. If the company hasn't learned how to manage its own data and solve why the data quality issues happened, the data will start going bad as soon as they leave. You need to learn how to manage your data. Your data is your responsibility

What you need to do is solve the problem. Find the root cause and unravel that issue. You need to figure out what went wrong with the data and fix it for good. It's not always a quick and easy process. You can think of it like a scavenger hunt. You hunt for it. You turn over some rocks. You look around some corners. It sometimes appears so obvious you can't believe it.

Once discovered, you can remediate. You might have to change coding or a process. You might need to talk to some employees or vendors. You also need to identify if anything else needs to change. You might find a data issue that is bigger than you expected and may impact months of past reporting. By solving it though, you've eliminated something to worry about. The alternative is giving yourself an operational process of fixing the same data repeatedly, which will be prone to error.

Think about comparing the root cause to plants. Plants have roots. The flowers, fruit, foliage, etc., are based on those roots. If the roots bring nourishment, the flowers, fruit, foliage, etc., will be improved. You also want that in your data. Bring in good data, which will improve your reports, analytics, and AI. If you find a problem, fix why it happened–the root cause. .

Data in Real Life–If There's One, There's Probably Another

In a new home, I had to provide the construction manager with a list of what needed to be fixed. Coming up with that list took a methodical approach. For things that I assumed were fine and ignored, then discovered I made a bad assumption, I had to be thorough in looking further. One day, I discovered that an interior door didn't latch. While I put it on the list, I also went to every room and checked every door. Sure enough, I added more doors to the list.

This scenario can be compared to data quality. Be proactive in looking for problems before your customers find them. The construction manager should have found these simple issues with my home. If you're not proactive and wait for your customer to alert you of a problem, not only do you look bad, but you're now scrambling to fix the problem for the customer.

But what do you do with this new information? Do you fix the problem the customer told you about, or do you also look to see if there's more the customer didn't find? Just like I had to check every door in my home, the construction manager should have checked when he came to fix one. Maybe you're alerted to an address with a missing ZIP Code. Be conscientious. Take the time to check all your addresses to see if there are other ZIP Codes you missed.

Data in Real Life—Do you Understand "Correct"?

A company sent me a document to sign, but there were inconsistencies with my name. They spelled it correctly at the top of the page and incorrectly at the bottom of the page. When I called customer care, they claimed it was correct.

Since it's my name, I felt more qualified in identifying what was correct. When I pointed out the inconsistency again, she claimed it was stored correctly and then blamed "the computer" for truncating part of my first name. She said it was too long. Most reasonable people know it's not that long, but truncating a name is an odd choice. In the worst-case scenario, maybe just use the first initial.

She really dug into her belief that "the computer" was correct and that she had no way to fix it. We clearly had different definitions of "correct."

In the end, it was escalated to her manager. He explained that IT could, should, and did fix the problem. It's possible it was a truncation issue. I'm more likely to believe that someone manually entered it wrong. This was a really easy problem to avoid. The name was right in one place, so they could have copied it if they had to keep it in multiple places. It was likely another data quality problem caused by humans.

Ten

Data Privacy

The first thing to understand about data privacy is what exactly it means. When someone says "data privacy," a lot of people hear "data security." Those are two different things, although both are important.

Think of data security as protecting the data from outside forces. This is where we think of hackers and data breaches. Technology can help protect data security.

Data privacy though is more about protecting the data from inside forces. We need to handle the data properly so we don't accidentally do something that exposes someone's data to people who shouldn't see it. This could be things like restricting everyone at a company from seeing a co-worker's medical information, not sending personnel records to an external vendor unless you know how they'll protect the data, or not showing customer information in a public webinar.

Working with Data Privacy

Data privacy is a hot topic because so many companies hold private data about us, and they need to protect it. We hear about it in the news when it hasn't been protected. Customers expect their data to be handled appropriately. Companies need to prevent data breaches and data privacy issues in general. Failure to follow privacy regulations hurts the company's reputation and fines can be significant.

The government can impose regulations around data privacy. However, even without that, it should be commonsense that we need to be good stewards of customer data or risk the customer relationship. You need to be monitoring for regulations. You can't be complacent and wait for someone to come and tell you there's a regulation you need to follow.

Data is all around us and you have to maintain the privacy of all of it. Is it in a database? Is it on a document? Is it on a post-it stuck to your monitor? Did you download it and store a copy on your personal laptop? Did you put data into an email and send it to someone? Is data hanging out in a garbage can? There's so much you need to be aware of. You might think you're doing something harmless, but people are trying to access the data for not-so-great reasons.

When you try to market to a customer or prospect, you need to understand what you can do with the data. Many people sign up, maybe for a discount or a contest, but that doesn't always mean you can do whatever you want with the data. Make sure you understand the law and respect the wishes of any "opt-out" preferences.

Global companies have the most difficulty because privacy is not universal. You need to understand the different privacy regulations. Even within the same country, like the US, the regulations can vary, such as varying by state. You have to consider not just where your business resides but where your customers are.

> If you have a data privacy issue, you need to confront it. Trying to hide it will just make it worse when people find out, and they always find out.

Data privacy is a very specialized subject. You don't want your company to be the next headline in the news. Some companies hire Chief Privacy Officers to be responsible for data privacy. In collaboration with the data governance organization, the right decisions can be made to protect the privacy of the data.

Data in Real Life–When I Say Don't Keep My Data, I Mean Don't Keep My Data

I pay a monthly invoice. The company sent me an email stating that it was ready and that I could view and pay online. I pay it via credit card. I do not store my credit card in my account for security reasons. I take the time to enter it every month so I have more control over my data.

One month, they emailed me that my invoice was ready. It was due the following week. The next day, they texted me that my invoice was ready. They had never done that before. It wasn't just a reminder. The text asked if I wanted to pay with my usual credit card, and they included the last four digits of the card number.

I checked my account, which confirmed that my credit card was not on file. When I paid my bill, I entered my credit card number because they didn't have it. And yet, the text accurately listed the last four digits.

We know they need the credit card information to process the payment. From a security perspective, we know there should be encryption and ways to protect data. From a privacy perspective, having that information to process a single payment does not give them the right to store it and use it later to send via text, unless you've specifically given them that permission. It gave me no confidence that my data was safe and validated that I made the right decision not to store my private data. Unfortunately, this was a utility company, so I had no option but to continue doing business with them.

Data in Real Life—Classified Documents

After some FBI classified documents were leaked online, they did an investigation to find out how it happened. Watching the news one night, I heard them say, "How did someone in IT have access to these classified documents that got leaked?" Well, that's not really something that surprised me. It wasn't the first leak and won't be the last.

Some employees need access to data the general public doesn't. Some IT employees need access to data the average employee doesn't. It's important to remember that just because you're an employee doesn't mean you're allowed to access all the data and do whatever you want with it. Companies need to have policies and processes around data privacy. People need to know what they can and can't do with the data–it needs to be monitored and enforced.

Eleven

Data Retention, Archiving, and Destruction

Your company will go through a lot of data over time, and you need to think about what you will do with it. You need to think about what data you retain, if you put any data into an archive, and when you think about destroying that data. There could be policies you write, but make sure you monitor those policies to see if they're being followed.

Decisions made once could change later, either because of business or regulation changes. Schedule a yearly review of your policies to see if anything needs to be updated.

Resist the urge to keep all data "just because" you might need it one day. Don't store it if it doesn't have a purpose and could put you at risk. There was a time when people kept everything because it was cheap to do so, but then you also found yourself knowing you had the data but unable to find it.

If you're storing data, remember where you put it. Even if you don't regularly use it, you have to be able to find it if needed for a legal case. Not being able to locate it isn't a great legal argument. Don't be like the time capsule people buried years ago and no one kept a record of its location.

Some state privacy laws say people can ask you what data you keep on them. The laws can go so far as to tell you the time constraint you have to comply. If you don't have the data clearly documented, you will have trouble complying in the required timeframe. Additionally, people can request that you remove all their data from your databases, often referred to as "the right to be forgotten." Again, is that something you'll be able to comply with?

If you might use the data in ten years, is it even going to be relevant then? Data sometimes doesn't age well. While we always like the idea of trending, trending only works if you have the same data set consistently.

When you consider retaining data, involve your lawyers. They will tell you how long you legally have to keep the data. There's a myth around keeping all data for the same timeframe, but your lawyers can give you the facts around what data and for how long. They will know because if there's a violation, they're the ones who have to plead your case.

Before you run out the door from the lawyers, they will talk to you about destroying data, which they generally care about more than retention. While some data needs to be kept for a certain period of time for legal reasons, it is also necessary to destroy data when it is no longer required. Keeping data you don't need to keep means that it will be available if there should be legal proceedings. The adage, "Would you want that read in open court?" applies.

Whoever Dies with the Most Data Wins

Have we turned into data hoarders? We fell in love with the idea of data and what it could tell us. But, have we gotten carried away? Do we know what we're doing with all that data? Have we started playing a game and whoever dies with the most data wins?

First we had data. Then we had big data. And don't forget the Internet of Things (IoT). We put the data into data lakes. We watched the lake turn into a swamp. We forgot what data we had and couldn't find data we were pretty sure was there. Data can be really powerful, but you still need to govern your big data. If you don't know what data you have, where it is, what it means, how good it is, and how to use it, you're not necessarily using it properly and could get unexpected results.

There was a time when you had to think carefully about whether or not you could afford to keep certain data or how long you could keep it. Then people got mesmerized hearing their IT departments tell them, "Disk space is cheap." People are now gathering lots of data but aren't always using it effectively.

> *Just because you <u>can</u> collect some data, doesn't*
> *necessarily mean you <u>should</u>.*

Get the right data and use it properly to benefit the company. Get rid of the data you don't need because it becomes noise and can distract you from your purpose, not to mention the potential privacy and security concerns around the data. Can you truthfully tell your legal department what's in your databases?

New data comes along in different ways. Some new data might be generated internally in your company. There might be some industry data sets available that you acquire. There might be some exciting research a consulting company has created for you. Either way, what is the cost? There might be a cost to purchase (or lease) the data, but that's not the full cost. Even internal data can have costs. The data might be most effective if it's integrated with other data you have, so you have to look into those integration costs. You might have to do some data cleansing before integration. You need to check the data quality. It's also probably not a one-time data load because you need to keep the data fresh, so you're looking at regular maintenance costs. And you're probably using staff with many other things to do.

Acquiring data might require you to create a cost/benefit analysis. What is the hypothesis you're trying to prove?

What problem are you trying to solve? What benefit will the data provide you? Are you effectively using the company's money for this project? Does the benefit outweigh the cost? Think about tangible and intangible benefits. Will this data help the company generate more income, or perhaps something like good will or a benefit to society?

In your rush to collect all the data, don't forget to govern it. Some people think that moving to a data lake means a looser type of environment. They think of greater flexibility and throw around words like "agile." The problem with that thinking is that if you don't start out governing your data from the beginning, it will be more difficult to govern it later. You still need controls so you can help inform people on what is available, help them get access, explain what the data is so they don't make erroneous assumptions, maintain compliant usage, verify data quality, etc. If you don't govern the data from the start, it's almost like an archaeological dig later figuring out what's in there and if you're violating any regulations.

> Data can be very powerful, but know what you will
> do with it so you don't wind up as the latest
> participant on the Hoarders TV show.

Data in Real Life—Where's That Retirement Money?

A large international bank was accused of losing some of its customers' retirement plans. The customers made deposits into retirement plans in the 1990s, but then made no additional deposits and did not monitor the status of the money. Nearing retirement, they claim the money is no longer there.

The bank went through a significant merger since the deposits were made in the 1990s. Although they say that the records no longer exist, they also seem to have proof that the customers withdrew the money years ago and the closed accounts no longer exist.

At the time of this writing, I don't know how this one turns out because it hasn't been resolved yet.

From the bank's perspective, the customers had withdrawn the funds, so they had no funds to maintain. Any merger they went through should have had financial transactions to prove that the money moved successfully from point A to point B, but the bank claims the money was withdrawn prior to the merger, so there were no financial transactions. Plus, the bank claims the withdrawals were 20-plus years ago. We know there's a need to keep financial data for a period of time, but does it need to be kept for over 20 years?

The data retention and destruction rules around this one would be interesting to see. Is there an expectation that a bank needs to keep transactions forever? Does a closed account exist for a period of time and then get deleted? If destruction can happen within 20 years, what happens if customers come along 20-plus years later assuming the data (i.e., money) has been retained because they forgot they withdrew it? It's like the bank has to prove the absence of data to explain what happened. When creating your own data retention and destruction rules, think if you would encounter similar situations after destruction.

Twelve

Testing Data

Testing data is so important, but it's something that people often forget. They might test an application to make sure all the buttons take the user to the correct spot, but you also have to test that the actions taken on the data yield the correct results. If you're moving data, was it moved correctly? If you're transforming data, was it transformed correctly? You need to validate data whenever you move or transform it.

People sometimes use "control totals" in testing. While this can be a good starting point, it's not a great ending point. For instance, do you celebrate victory if you received $10,000 in transactions, moved the data to another database, and still had $10,000? You better not! You need to check the details. Maybe that $10,000 was made up of $4,000 for Bob Smith and $6,000 for a different person also named Bob Smith. If you get confused and give all $10,000 to one of the Bob Smiths, you'll have one unhappy Bob Smith and maybe one really happy Bob Smith.

Another thing people sometimes do is use "thresholds." Maybe the threshold is 95%. They move $10,000. The new database doesn't get $10,000, but the number is at least 95% of $10,000. And they celebrate victory. Really? Before celebrating, ensure the business is comfortable using a threshold like that. If it's money and it's Bob Smith's money, he's not going to be happy with a threshold. He wants his whole $10,000.

Take the time to properly test your data. It's your last line of defense before you send your data out into the world.

When Bad Applications Happen to Good People

It's always sad when people spend so much effort in developing an application and then treat the data like a second-class citizen. Data needs to be tested as much, or more, than an application. You can have the fastest application and nicest front-end, but if the data behind it is bad, what's the point?

> *I've encountered a lot of people who don't know how to test data. They can test an application front-end to ensure that dropdowns do drop down and radio buttons go on and off. They can test an application back-end to ensure data displays where it should. But, did they thoroughly check that the right data is displaying and that the data is being transformed properly?*

Your data should be checked at every stage of data movement. When you receive the data, make sure you got the right data. When you combine data with other data or perform calculations, make sure it was transformed correctly. When you display it in an application or on a report, make sure the end result is right. If you're thoroughly testing the data prior to implementation, you have less to worry about in production. A company shouldn't need to have a huge data quality team if they're following good data management practices like this.

A typical testing process has test cases where you identify your expected results and then compare them to the actual test results. The same goes for testing data. Identify what data goes in and the expected result, and then determine the actual results. You need to create that controlled environment where you know what you're sending through and what it should look like on the other end.

Where does the data come from? Some people run a subset of production data through the tests. This is a good place to start because you have test data and don't have to create it from scratch. The problem though is that your subset of production data does not necessarily include every test case you have. You might still need to create some data from scratch to properly test your data. If you only use "real" data, that probably means you're only testing good data, and you also want to see what happens if the application gets bad data. Also, what did the business tell you about the problems? You want to make sure that your test cases cover the issues the business has. When you deliver the application to your business sponsors, you want to be able to confidently tell them that the application works properly, rather than it's in the "ballpark" and maybe pretty close to being right, only to fail in your first production run. How embarrassing.

When people are updating an application or replacing an application, it always surprises me during testing when they compare test results to the current application. You're choosing to change the application, so that means that something is wrong that you want to fix. That means that future state should not necessarily match current state. Again, you need to create the proper test cases and identify what the data should be, which may be different from the current state.

Remember to include business people in testing. From a business perspective (not to be confused with the technical perspective), they should be telling you what they want tested. No matter how much time you spend with them beforehand, it is not unusual for business people to see something in the testing process and then say, "What if ...?" Those what-ifs, although they can feel annoying, are very helpful because it tells you that they're getting it and feel the accountability for getting it right. If no what-ifs come out of testing, then you can probably tell they're just going through the motions, following the instructions, and don't understand it.

> It's important to take a disciplined approach and thoroughly test your data before implementing an application. Testing is the last line of defense before releasing something into production. Don't shortchange it. Be careful, thorough, and accurate. Don't make it a half attempt and cross your fingers hoping that production doesn't have data you didn't bother to test for.

Data in Real Life—You Did Not Win the Powerball

A man checked his Powerball numbers online and saw he had won $340 million.

When he took his ticket in, he was told there had been a mistake and he didn't win anything.

The lottery had been conducting some testing and had accidentally posted numbers that matched this man's ticket. They didn't discover the error for three days.

This is a great example of how bad an idea it is to test in production. You need a test environment, but some people try to shortcut it by doing something in production. They probably thought they could get away with it, but it happened that someone checked when they had test data posted. Worse, it wasn't just test data but data that looked real. It was so real that it happened to match someone's ticket. When something like that happens, it throws the whole process into question. How many times have people not claimed the winning ticket because they checked online when test data was posted?

Thirteen

Analytics

E veryone wants analytics, but you need to make sure you're building the analytics over a foundation of good data. Building that foundation takes time. You can't cut corners. If you have no information about the data, you shouldn't assume it's ready to use. Work in an environment of governed data where the data you receive is acceptable for use in analytics. If the data isn't sufficient, you could be making questionable decisions on the data. Sound mathematical techniques are of little value if applied against substandard data, leaving the analytics and insights worthless.

Follow an analytics strategy aligned with the business strategy. Why are analytics important to you? What goals are you trying to achieve with analytics? You need to develop a strategy that is specific and actionable. You need more than just a short elevator speech. Unfortunately, the data doesn't magically speak to you. You need to have an idea of what you're trying to achieve.

When working with analytics, you often develop user stories. Are you trying to find a way to detect and prevent fraud? Are you trying to increase the effectiveness of marketing campaigns? Are you trying to do something to gain a competitive advantage? You don't know where to direct your efforts without knowing the problem you're trying to solve. You want to develop a theory, acquire the data, and test the hypothesis. You need to flush out your story, identify the results you expect to achieve, and understand the ROI. If the cost of developing the analytics and implementing the solution is more than the value you expect to get from the analytics, it might not be worth undertaking it.

When you work on analytics, you might develop some sophisticated calculations. It's probably not a one-time activity. You've probably created something that could be repeated in the future. For that reason, make sure that you document those calculations. Think of governing your analytics in a very similar way to governing your data.

When working with analytics, it's important to remember that data can change over time. This means that your analytics are not static and your analytics may need to change over time. If new data comes in that you hadn't considered when you developed your analytics, it may impact your calculations. Additionally, at the very least, refreshed data means re-running your analytics.

The main thing to remember about analytics is to take action. This is not an academic exercise. While it can be a fun challenge to develop analytics, you need to act on what you learned from the analytics to develop the insights you need to move the business forward.

With analytics, always remember that good analytics requires good data. Know what problem you're trying to solve before undertaking analytics. Analytics can quickly go down that black hole you get into, similar to watching YouTube videos always leads to cat videos, but if you focus your activities, analytics can be very effective in solving business problems.

Analytics Governance

People hopefully understand data governance. The concept of analytics governance isn't as widely known, but the principles are the same.

You don't want to leave one technical person alone to generate all the analytics. They need the input from the business. The business doesn't have the technical knowledge to generate the analytics and the technical team doesn't have the business knowledge. Through collaboration, they can generate the needed analytics.

Another part of the collaboration is the validation that the thought process of the analytic is correct. I've seen phone numbers go wrong so often with analytics. People look at the area code and assume that shows where the person lives, when in reality, it shows where the person obtained the phone. I don't know if this is because some people just genuinely don't realize that you don't have to change your phone number when you move, or you want a phone number in a particular area code for certain reasons, or maybe they live in a country where this doesn't happen.

Whatever the issue, making an erroneous assumption about the data, and in this case, something as simple as the phone's area code, can throw off analytics.

You need to document the analytics. You need to understand the data you're using to know it's the right data. That comes through the definitions and the data lineage. The analytics probably involve a calculation, so document that. There might be restrictions on how to use the analytics or who to share with. You're working your way through the same issues you talk about with data governance, but you're applying it to analytics.

Analytics governance is not the same as data governance. Although the principles are similar, you're applying them against different things. I have seen companies have separate data governance and analytics governance organizations. Some people try to combine them, but they have a separate focus. For instance, the data governance organization might discuss a change in customer definition. The analytics people don't need to be in that discussion, although they do need to be informed of the results. By keeping the organizations separate but sharing the results, you haven't bored them with having to sit through the whole debate.

Data Management versus Data Analysis

Many companies want to get into analytics and think all they need to do is hire a data analyst or data scientist. Those are the right people to perform analytics but don't forget that your first step is getting good data in place to help your analytics people.

Data and analytics use different skill sets. While analytics people can be highly skilled in using the data to get analytics (and hopefully, insights), they are not a replacement for highly skilled people in data management.

Make sure you're hiring the right people. I've seen companies pile on the analysts because they need more people to write reports, and their analysts are swamped. However, the real issue is that they're not giving their analysts good data, so they waste time trying to understand data issues before starting their reports. Data management is needed first so your analysts have good data and can get the job done that they know how to do and enjoy.

Analysts need to understand the data they've been given to work with. You don't want to be like the community that got lots of government funding because of their high population compared to surrounding communities, only to find out later that the higher population was because that community contained the jails. The population was higher, but they were all within a certain facility instead of being a community that needed more money for highways, schools, etc.

Consider a simple example where an analyst researches customers based on city. You want that analyst to have the necessary data to start working. The analyst will get inaccurate results if the data contains misspelled city names. What happens next if the analyst first checks the data and finds the misspellings? Maybe the analyst modifies the data, but is it done correctly? For instance, if you mix up something like "St John" and "St John's," you get very different cities. Does the analyst really know enough to fix the data correctly? But what does this "fix" even mean? If the analyst has just updated data in an Excel spreadsheet, the data that everyone else uses hasn't changed, and the data that the analyst will use in the future hasn't changed either. This means the analyst has generated a lifelong task of "fixing" data. This is not the analyst's skill set and is not what they want to do. If there isn't a data governance lead, they get stuck fixing data issues because no one else is doing it. They even generated their own term for it–data wrangling, and that isn't a compliment.

What should happen is that the analyst should alert the data governance lead that there is a data problem so that the data governance lead can get the source of the data issue fixed. Maybe people are typing data incorrectly. Maybe a vendor is sending data incorrectly. Unless you fix the source of the problem, you have a constant fixing task and you're making the wrong people perform this task. The data governance lead has the expertise and authority to fix this data once and for all so it won't keep happening.

I heard someone describe data like laundry–comparing cleaning data to constantly doing the laundry. I don't think I like that analogy. I might be constantly washing the same towels, but I hope I'm not constantly cleaning the same data. When you look at it that way, you're handling your data incorrectly. If you're constantly fixing the same data problem, you're not addressing why there are problems with the data in the first place. Maybe someone's typing in bad data. Maybe a vendor is sending bad data. Maybe someone coded a calculation wrong. Fix the ultimate problem so you don't have to keep fixing it again and again. The same can't be said for your towels. Unless you keep buying new ones, you will have to keep washing them. If we wait until the analysts find the problems in the data, they're going to be the ones constantly doing the same laundry over and over again.

Data, Analytics, and Insights

Many people talk about analytics and insights without knowing exactly what these things mean. They've heard the company will benefit but don't know how to get there. They might try to throw money at it and hire talented data scientists hoping it will magically happen, but that's not how it works.

It all starts with data. You have data about your customers. You collect data from doing business with your customers. You apply mathematical techniques to your data to obtain analytics. You then apply business knowledge to your analytics to obtain insights. Those insights will ideally provide you with insightful information about your business that will allow you to take action. This might be an insight around payment trends that can help you work with customers before problems occur. This might be an insight on something new happening in the industry requiring your attention.

To understand data, analytics, and insights, think about a painting. Stand inches from a painting and you see brushstrokes and dots of paint. It's just a bunch of stuff without any context that doesn't make sense to you. That's data. Now step a few feet back and look at the painting again. At this point, you're starting to see forms take shape. You might see people or buildings, but there's something there beyond those brushstrokes and dots. Think of that like your analytics. Step further back again. You're able to see that painting in all its glory. Your emotion takes over and you can read something into it that you didn't initially see. It's not about dots anymore. It's not necessarily about that single building. It's about what the image as a whole is telling you. It could be different from the artist's statement that went along with the painting. Those are insights.

Applying business logic to analytics to get insights is essential. What you don't want is to stop at analytics. Mathematically, you can often find a way to interpret the data to get it to say what you want it to say. How many times have we seen questionable statistics in the media? Make sure that business subject matter experts support the data scientists in applying their knowledge to the analytics they see. They'll be able to work together to interpret those analytics properly.

You have to make sure that you have the right people working together to turn data into analytics and then into insights.

Data and the Cookie Analogy

We've all tried those sugar cookies left on the table outside the conference room. What are these things? What do they taste of? Do they even have sugar in them?

Then there's Grandma's sugar cookies, or at least someone's Grandma. Tasty. You wait all year for them at Christmas. But they have the same name as those cookies outside the conference room. What happened?

Think ingredients. Grandma's cookies have fresh ingredients and maybe things that are hard to find. The leftover conference room cookies probably have artificial ingredients, were made to last, and you don't even know where they came from.

Think of those ingredients as your data and the cookies as your analytics. You might still get cookies without good ingredients, but not necessarily good ones. And without good data, you don't get good analytics and AI.

CDO or CDAO?

First came the Chief Data Officer, CDO. Then people started talking about the Chief Data and Analytics Officer, CDAO. Do we need both roles?

The creation of the CDO role was a great idea. It recognized the importance of data. It recognized that data was a function in and of itself, separate from the business and technology. For some companies, this is a starting point when they have not been taking care of data and need to give it more attention. They need to get their data house in order to have success actually using that data. They might not be ready to jump into analytics until they have data under control.

Once they are ready for analytics, they can then create another role for a Chief Analytics Officer (CAO). Working closely with the CDO, the CAO knows someone is working on the data so it's ready for the analytics.

Data and analytics need two different skill sets. Each has a different purpose. They're related though. Analytics need data to be successful. Data can exist without analytics. You can easily argue that having data itself is not necessarily worthwhile–it's the analytics that manifests the value of that data.

The problem is that if you give all your attention to the analytics, which is the bright shiny object people look at, you're not giving enough attention to your data. Data is the foundation of analytics. Your analytics are worthless if you're not taking care of your data.

If you think you can skip having a CDO and just have a CDAO, then you probably haven't shown the value data brings to a company and its analytics. When analytics always overshadow data, you'll never get good data.

Ideally, you can have a CDO focus on data and a CAO focus on analytics. Each can report to the CEO, so be on the same level as the other Chiefs, like the Chief Technology Officer and Chief Marketing Officer. Trying to combine them into a CDAO can be too much for one person and won't give enough attention to each one.

Just because a new idea comes along does not mean you have to jump on their bandwagon. There may have been a reason someone suggested a new concept and it might not apply to you.

Data in Real Life—My DNA Changed?

Years ago, I did one of those genealogy DNA tests—not because I didn't know, but because I thought it would be fun. There was one country that wasn't listed, although it seemed to be unfortunately mixed with another country. Why? It's all because of what data was available. People in that country didn't need the DNA test. They just know. Also, many of them had already done a DNA test through a local company.

Over the years, people in that particular country have started taking this test and I've seen my DNA results change. Obviously, I haven't changed, but the data set has. With proper representation, this country can now be included in my DNA results.

Remember that when you're using your data. If you don't have the right data, you won't get the right results. It's not always about errors in the data. It can be about what data sets you have available to you.

Fourteen

Technology

I call it the triad that acts on data–people, process, and technology. In that order. Technology is more about accelerating the progress of the people and processes. Technology alone is not the driver and cannot manage data.

Too many people think you can just buy a tool and that's it. I'm not sure where that idea comes from. I'm assuming it has something to do with people erroneously putting the management of data into IT, where we know it's not uncommon to buy tools.

Think about making dinner. You can have all the ingredients, utensils, and oven. Without a person following the recipe, you don't have dinner. Just the existence of an oven isn't getting you there.

Think of a company as having three things, another triad–business, technology, and data. Data is a separate function. It's not part of the business and it's not part of technology. It is its own function. Understanding that helps you identify where data sits within a company, which is not in the business or in technology.

There are lots of tools on the market that can help with data management. You can buy data quality tools, metadata tools, MDM tools, etc. Are there data governance tools? I tend to think not. If we think of data governance as more of the people side where we establish a data governance organization, there really isn't a tool for that. There are tools that can help you run the organization, such as workflow tools and document repositories. Some tools cover multiple capabilities, so they can be considered data management tools.

As much as we have data quality tools, there needs to be a reality check. You don't point them at a database and they magically fix what's wrong. You still need to tell the tool what to look for—it should be looking for problems based on how you define data quality, not how someone outside your business thinks you should define data quality. You also still need to fix the problems—the tool won't go into your databases and programs to fix the errors it thinks there are. And remember to fix the source of the problem—determine what caused it and fix it there so it doesn't keep happening.

There was a time when everyone was talking about self-service. The idea was to put access to the data in the hands of the people needing it so that they didn't have to keep asking someone in IT to extract some data for them. That vision hasn't always aged well. Some companies have been more successful than others. Some have found that the users of self-service don't understand the data well enough to know if they're looking at the right data. Is the problem that users need more education and better documentation? Or is the problem that the users have access to tools that are just more sophisticated than the average user needs? If a marketing person needs to sit through a week-long class to understand how to get the data they need each month, you might have to determine if this is cost effective.

> *A tool fixes a technology problem. Data management fixes a data problem. You can't tool your way out of a data problem.*

Are Data Tools Magical?

Have you ever installed a magical data tool—a tool that will fix every data problem you have? It always surprises me to talk to people who think that data tools are plug-and-play and they just need to install the right tool so all their data problems will magically disappear. Maybe they think installing an MDM tool will solve all master data issues overnight or a data quality tool will solve all quality issues. There are some great tools out there, but you still have to configure them correctly and use them the right way. Without that, you've installed "something" and it's going to do what it was programmed to do. If you configure the tool to merge certain records, it will merge the records that meet your criteria, so you better make sure you give the tool the right instructions. Sometimes, a tool can feel magical because you had so many problems before that were eliminated when you installed it, but we all know that there isn't a magical leprechaun (or my personal favorite, the Icelandic huldufólk) sitting in a corner fixing our data for us.

You need the right expectations when you decide to use a tool. Understand what the tool can and can't do for you. Expectations are often where people go wrong. They might think a tool can do everything. In reality, the tool often has some great capabilities, but then you need another tool to do something else. If you don't fully understand the tool's capabilities, you might be trying to configure it in some twisted way to do something it was not meant to do. Also, the tool might point out potential data problems to you and you still need to solve those issues. It would be horrible if the tool was pointing out that some data was erroring out and you never bothered to check the error log.

I've seen expectation issues from both the business and IT sides. The business might not understand exactly what they need, but they heard about things like MDM or data quality tools. They ask their IT department to get one. If they haven't fully explained the problem, IT is looking for a generic tool that might fix the problem but not necessarily solve the actual business problems. The business needs to take the time to explain the issue and what problems the tool will need to solve.

You need to allow time to understand what the tool can do, collect business requirements, configure the tool correctly, test it thoroughly, and then implement it. The tool will function based on how you configured it, so you need to ensure you configure it correctly. Even with thorough testing, there might be some test scenarios you never dreamed up, so you may need to review your configuration on an interim basis after implementation. And make sure you truly use scenarios that test all the business problems. Don't try to shortcut things by taking a subset of production data and crossing your fingers that every single problem is in that subset. You need to do your due diligence so that the business has confidence in the tool you installed for them.

IT also needs to know where their strengths lie. When you start getting into sophisticated and complex data issues, the skill set may not reside within the IT department, and you may need to hire consultants to configure the tools properly. These days, many companies choose not to have specialized skills within IT, but use consultants on an interim basis when needed.

> *The other key component of data tools is data governance. You can buy a tool, but your tool investment will wither and die if you don't have the appropriate data governance.*

If you lack data governance, build it in parallel with your tool implementation. The people you recruit for your data governance organization will help you define the requirements for the tool, test it, perhaps use it in production, benefit from it, and potentially deal with operational issues. These are the people you need. After implementing the tool, expand the reach of your data governance organization beyond what you accomplished with the single tool. You can expand on what you govern and recruit even more people.

When you need to configure the tool, whether in-house or with consultants, the team needs to work with the business people you identified in your data governance organization who understand the business rules. Tool configuration, like data governance, must be business-led and technology-supported. It's important to involve the business to get the right rules implemented. Often, IT people might think they understand the rules and try to configure the tool themselves to save time for business people. While that thought comes from people trying to be helpful, you'll probably miss some business rules and implement some incorrect ones, so make sure you take the time to work with the true decision makers.

You need to think about how the tool will be used in production. Who will be hands-on with it and who will be using reports coming from the tool? The people in your data governance organization need to be the ones who come together to figure out what actions you're going to take. If a data quality tool identifies potential issues, the data governance organization should be involved in reviewing the issues, making decisions, and taking action. Likewise, data governance team members need to respond to issues coming from an MDM tool.

Tools can be powerful, but they will do exactly what you tell them to do. That's how computer programming works. Tools don't live at the end of rainbows beside pots of gold. Remember to engage tools with eyes wide open, be realistic about what they can do for you, communicate with your stakeholders so they know what to expect, use data governance, and implement correctly.

Fifteen

Living with Data

M anaging data is not a trivial task. It becomes an operational task to ensure that the right people get the right data on time and understand how to use it compliantly.

Change Management

If you have not been following data management practices and then try to, you will probably benefit from change management. It can be a shift in the way people think and you need to make sure people understand the benefits of the change.

From the business side, the business needs to recognize that they are experts in the business and they make the business decisions. They also know the business rules. They have to communicate clearly to IT and share those decisions and rules. They have to take part in testing to check that implementation is accurate. No single person will make all the data decisions, but you can build a data governance organization to include all affected parties in decisions.

IT needs to recognize that they are not experts in the business, nor are they expected to be, and they have to defer to the business on business decisions. They are responsible for the technical implementation of business decisions and rules. If they don't receive clear direction from the business, they must ask for it rather than make assumptions. They need to involve the business in testing so everything is approved before implementation.

Communication is important, with plenty of lead time. Schedule activities so people can plan accordingly. One small change might impact other things that also need to change. Create clear documentation that makes sense when you have to refer back to it.

This is also more than just an initial implementation. There will be changes over time, whether because there are business changes or because you found errors. The business and IT involvement continues with change management after implementation in an operational mode.

The Reality of Managing Data

Whether you're talking about data governance, data management, or information management, you need good data people who have an understanding of both concepts and reality. If someone just understands things from a theoretical standpoint, they can have a problem understanding how those concepts fit into reality. If someone just understands how to implement a tool, they too can have problems understanding how what they do fits into the reality of business.

Throughout my career, I've seen pretty much everything. I've worked as an employee and a consultant, and I've also been a client of consulting companies. I've done things without tool budgets, meaning we understood how to create a solution by understanding the problem and how to fix it. We could bring in data from multiple sources and reconcile it into a "golden record" when that buzzword hadn't been created yet. It was just the right way to handle data. It's common sense.

There are lots of good tools these days, but people don't always understand how to use them and configure them properly. They might understand how to technically implement the tool but don't really understand how the tool truly impacts people. Business people and technical people need to work together to understand the business rules and get them technically implemented. This is typically why we often talk about data governance not being about a technical implementation. You can always find someone who knows a tool. You can't always find someone who knows how to blend the tool into the reality of the situation. Plus, it's not uncommon to have to write a business case for funding, so you need to understand those impacts for your business case.

Data quality is one of those things that seems to have a lot of variability in skills. There are a lot of different aspects of data quality and you can find a lot of people who can put together a good PowerPoint presentation explaining data quality. But you have to follow through with that PowerPoint. Beyond the concepts of data quality, you have real people dealing with real problems with the data. Those people need someone who can identify and then fix those problems. That could involve multiple people–someone working with the business to understand what quality means to them and identifying where the issues are in the data (e.g., a source data problem, a transformation problem, a calculation problem, a reporting problem) and someone who can dig into program code to see where it went wrong and fix it.

MDM also requires variability in skills. I've seen smart people get trained in implementing an MDM tool and they definitely know how to configure that tool. However, what often gets missed is understanding why you're implementing the tool in the first place. If the person doing the implementation does not come from a data background, they might not understand their impact on the business. The business probably has a whole host of problems causing bad data and they can't trust the data they're working with. You need to identify those problems and configure the tool to prevent them. An MDM implementation can solve problems but needs to be implemented with a full understanding of the impact on the company. Once implemented, it is also important to remember the magnitude of what you've done. I've seen people go into the MDM tool and tweak rules (in production) to better master the data, not realizing that they have now changed the production data without any communication of the impact. They made the change thinking they were helping but didn't consider the ramifications. Were financial statements impacted? Was compensation affected? What information was based on the wrong data that they "fixed"? Did they even test it first? Was the data right before or is it right now? Who needs to know about this?

Managing data is not about throwing a tool at a problem. While a tool can help accelerate progress, it will probably create a bigger mess if you don't understand what it can do for you. We managed data before some of these tools came along. It might have taken us a little longer, but we understood and fixed the problem. When the tools came along, we could apply that knowledge and the tools helped us. Similarly, if an MDM tool has the wrong rules, it will follow them. It can't read your mind. If you don't understand the problem and misuse the tool, it will do what you told it to, even if you made a mistake.

The reality of managing data is that you need to understand the implications of your decisions. This is not some conceptual pie-in-the-sky theory. Decisions impact data, data impacts information, and information impacts people. This is why a lot of us talk about "information management" and not just "data management."

Metrics

People sometimes choose to define metrics to measure their data management capabilities. They follow the adage, "You can't manage what you can't measure." This allows them to monitor progress over time. If you choose to do this, make sure you understand what you're getting into and make sure you choose your metrics wisely.

Make sure people don't try to game the system.

Unfortunately, metrics sometimes lead to the wrong behaviors. For instance, you want good definitions for your data elements. This isn't an academic exercise. Tracking a metric for how many data elements have definitions isn't going to be useful if it means people will write anything. Worse, you might choose to automate checking if there is a value in the definition field, so people will enter a space or a period to get past that challenge. If you instead have definitions validated and then don't record them as "done" until the data governance organization approves them, you can trust your metric a bit more.

The thought of metrics sometimes scares people. They might think they're being watched and measured. They might think they're going to be evaluated and their salary impacted. They might think you're setting them up to be fired if they miss a number. Be upfront on what your plan is for metrics.

Another consideration is what you will do with the metrics once you have them. You don't want just to put them on a report and file it away somewhere. Communicate your findings and take any necessary actions.

If the metrics aren't showing the results you want,
you need to figure out how to improve them.

An example of this can be shown in a city that installed speed zone cameras. Their goal was to stop speeding in certain areas. People caught speeding were mailed a fine, so the residents thought it was all about money. After making a ton of money and being hit by the wrath of the public, the Mayor declared success because they were catching fewer people speeding over time. However, if he had looked a little further into it, he would have realized the behavior changes that resulted from his metric. The speed zone cameras were catching fewer people because fewer people were taking those streets. Instead, people were taking alternate routes and there were increased traffic complaints from people living on the side streets. While he may have reduced speeding in certain areas, he moved the problem to other areas.

If you decide you need metrics, pick the right ones. People often immediately gravitate to measuring data quality. That's fine, except it's only one of many capabilities. If measuring is important to you, you really need to think through all the capabilities. Think what will provide the most business value and move you in the right direction.

Purchasing Data

There's so much data these days and many companies choose to purchase data from other companies to enhance what they have. Or at least, that's what they think. You must understand what you're getting if you choose to do this.

If you're paying money for something, you want something good, so check into the quality of the data. Is the company following good data management practices? Are they guaranteeing their product? Are they willing to make changes if you find some bad (or at least suspicious) data?

Again with the good data management practices, are they providing you with metadata? Are there descriptions for all the data you're getting? Are they good descriptions? Do you understand what it all means?

How often are you getting the data? Is this a one-time occurrence or are you getting regular data feeds from the company?

What happens when you get the data? Does the communication end or do they help you understand how you can integrate it with your current data to make it more useful to you?

Can you integrate the data? Understand the data contract and what you're allowed to do with the data. Depending on the data set, the vendor might be concerned about you trying to do certain things with the data, such as reverse engineering. They might not want you to discover their secrets!

Are you really purchasing this data? Although people talk about purchasing data, that's not always the case. Particularly when there are recurring data feeds, this is often a lease situation. Just like an apartment lease, this gives you the ability to use the data for the time limit identified in the contract.

LIVING WITH DATA • 193

Are there any data restrictions? Vendors might let you do anything you want with the data once you pay them, or they might place restrictions on the data. You might be able to share the data with anyone in your company, but can only share with consultants after you've first asked permission and perhaps documented it in writing. The vendor might never let you share the data with someone they consider a competitor. There also might be restrictions on sharing the data outside the country, which is especially important if you're a global company or use a cloud server in another country.

What happens when the contract ends? This is important to consider when you first start getting the data. You have to think that you might not keep renewing the contract in perpetuity, so something will happen in the future when the contract ends. Think of it like a prenup where you protect yourself in case there's a breakup. Some contracts say you have to return the data. I always find that funny. How are you "returning" data? The data is stored somewhere and possibly in multiple places. It's not like someone gave you a binder of data printed on paper and you can just hand back the binder. What they're talking about, obviously, is removing the data from your databases. Check if the contract requires them to come on-site to check your databases or if they'll just trust you if you tell them you deleted it. Some companies might allow you to keep data in an archived database as long as there is nothing in the current operational database, but make sure you understand the terms. If you took the data and integrated it into other databases, you probably would have massive referential integrity issues if you removed this data. What happens to any analytics or insights you gained from this data? Does the company allow you to keep those? The data strategy you had when you started the contract might be different when you ended the contract.

Understanding data contracts is typically something that falls under your data governance organization. There might be a data governance lead who works hand-in-hand with the lawyers to understand the conditions of the contract and communicate clearly to the rest of the organization.

Where Data Fits

> *If you have a data problem and buy the best tool your money can buy, you've solved a technical problem. If you have a data problem and hire the best analyst your money can afford, you've solved a skills problem. If you have a data problem, you need to solve the data problem the right way, with people who have data management skills. Then you can hire the right analyst and buy the right tool. Solve the right problem, not a generic problem.*

The question is always asked about where data belongs. People try to put data under existing parts of the company. It might be IT, finance, risk, compliance, marketing, or any other random area. It sometimes comes down to who has the problem and who has the budget.

I've seen marketing struggle to get communications out because of bad customer data, so they spearhead the effort. That's great, but practically everyone in the company uses customer data, so they have to make sure it doesn't become an isolated effort. I've seen it fall under finance, particularly when a company is struggling with accurate regulatory reporting because of bad data. I've seen it fall under risk or compliance, usually because the company failed an audit.

While I don't agree with the placements in the prior paragraph, I can get on board with them when the company is smaller, they're just starting out, and they seem to be open to doing the right thing and be willing to change in the future. The company culture tends to dictate how accepting people are of working together. If the effort is being led through marketing and they need to collaborate with sales and IT, many people are completely willing to do that.

What I have a difficult time getting behind is when the company puts data under IT. Many companies will try this when they're new to working with data. They think that if IT already supports the databases, it probably fits. The problem with putting it under IT is that people think data is technical and just need to buy a tool to fix it. They forget that the business plays a huge role in data. Not only do they use it, but they understand the business rules around it. Since IT is often sheltered and working on very specialized things that come with sophisticated skills, the business isn't always involved. That can lead too often to thinking IT will just handle this too.

The way I look at it is that data is its own function in the company. You have finance, marketing, IT, etc. And you have data. If you have a CTO reporting to the CEO, you also need a CDO reporting to the CEO. They have to be on an equal playing field. That's the only way that data will get the attention it needs to help the company be successful.

Data Risk Management—Saving People from Themselves

These days, it doesn't take much to hear about malicious external hacking attacks against companies, later followed by another email about a class action lawsuit and free credit monitoring services. There are technical considerations companies need to take to prevent these attacks, but also prevent the "softer" attacks—the attacks coming internally, often from people trying to be "helpful." Sometimes, people try to be helpful to others and don't think through the impact of their actions. Sometimes, processes need to be put into place to enforce "commonsense." This is what I call saving people from themselves.

Government regulations—There are regulations that apply to specific industries or countries. There are regulations that your data governance lead needs to be aware of, but that information needs to be shared with the appropriate people. Not everyone reads data literature (really?!), so we need to share that information. GDPR is something many people talk about, but there are others. If someone doesn't know that they're not allowed to share data outside their country, they could very easily do that. We have so many global companies, and it's easy to want to help a co-worker by sharing data. Just make sure there aren't any regulations in place preventing it. Global companies can also struggle to streamline activities and have skill sets isolated in certain countries. When decisions like that are made, they have to be made with the full understanding of what the company can do with the data so regulations aren't accidentally violated.

Sharing data–If you want to share data, do you know if you're allowed to? Many people use data all the time and don't think about where it came from. Ideally, you've created data lineage for your data, so you know where it comes from. People don't always realize that the data in your database doesn't always come from one of your company's applications. If the data was acquired from another company, it was probably "leased", even though a lot of people erroneously talk about "buying" it. If it was leased, you need to understand your data contracts and what they allow you to do with the data. The contract might allow you to share the data with anyone you want, or it might place restrictions. Those restrictions could be about either asking permission (and waiting for it to be granted!), or it could be as restrictive as not allowing the data to be shared with competitors. If your company works with consultants, whether independent or a large company, you might be subject to restrictions in the contracts. This is another place where the data governance lead comes in. You don't want to waste people's time by having lots of people picking through page-upon-page of legal contracts, so let your data governance lead and lawyers do that. There should be specific processes and perhaps templates in place so people understand what they need to do to share data. Your contracts might require a non-disclosure agreement to share verbal information and a third-party agreement to share data.

Storing data–Do you know where you're storing your data? Did you get caught up in the cloud? Just make sure that you're storing your data compliantly. If you're under regulations that the data needs to be stored in a particular country and you're using the cloud, make sure you know where the cloud server is. It doesn't sit in some fluffy spot in the sky–there's a physical server in a real country, and you have to know where if you're subject to restrictions on the location of your data.

Marketing–If you're sending marketing communications, do you know how to do that compliantly? We've all seen emails with an "unsubscribe" button at the bottom. It's not a coincidence that so many emails have that; they're following the CAN-SPAM law. However, you need to know what countries you're marketing in. Just within North America, Canada and the US have taken very different approaches. Canada has an "opt-in" approach, whereby you have to choose to receive emails from the company. The US took an "opt-out" approach–essentially, a company can send you whatever they want and you have to choose to unsubscribe.

Data retention and destruction–Data destruction is one of my favorites. So many people have had it drilled into their heads that "disk space is cheap" and we can store ALL the data. Plus, you often want to have as much data as possible if you're looking at trending. Make sure though that your data retention and destruction policy is created with the support of your legal department. Often, lawyers will tell you how long you must keep the data, but then follow that statement up with telling you to destroy the data after it has been kept for the required length of time. Companies don't want to hide information, but they sometimes want to make sure that the company doesn't go overkill with the data and potentially expose the company to legal action at some point in the future. If the data is available, it could be pulled into legal proceedings, even if it's outside the time period.

The bottom line—It's nice to think about working in a collaborative environment and being helpful to your co-workers. You just need to ensure that your helpfulness doesn't put the company at risk through data misuse. The data governance lead has the role of helping to save people from themselves and prevent these problems.

Storytelling

People talk about storytelling or data storytelling, but what does it mean? There are two scenarios. You might need one or the other, or both, depending on what you're attempting to do. Are you trying to tell the story of the data? Or are you trying to tell a story with data?

If you're trying to tell the story of the data, you're either trying to explain something that's wrong and needs to be fixed, or you're trying to build confidence in the data. The story might be that customer data comes in from multiple places and you need business help to determine what's right. The story might explain a calculation you're performing so people understand that the report they're receiving is correct. You're going into detail because that's what the audience needs.

If you're trying to tell a story with data, you're using results to show something. In this case, your audience doesn't need all the details. They're coming in with the assumption that you know what you're doing and have correctly performed all the hocus pocus that's needed. The story might show where most customers are from or the sales trends over the last year. You're using data to show a story, which might help decide where to focus sales activities or what products should be candidates for retirement.

In terms of telling that story, you might have to start small and build incrementally. Stop at each interval to make sure people understand before moving on to the next step. You might have to use a subset of data so people don't get overwhelmed. Pictures and diagrams can be very helpful.

Think of a regular story. What if you were writing a novel? You might start out with a premise or plot, give the background, walk through the trip you took, and then get to the conclusion. Can you fashion your data story in the same manner? Be clear and leave the audience without questions.

Data people are often thought of as translators, which is what you need in storytelling. You need that person who can understand both the business and IT, and translate what one says so that it can be understood by the other. The story that's told depends on the audience. Some need to read the whole book and some just need the last page.

You might need to tell your data's story in degrees. It might be screaming for help and you're not listening.

An address is wrong. Maybe you're trying to mail marketing materials. The prospect never asked for it, never received it, and is unaware there was an issue. The company sent it hoping to make a sale. They might be disappointed it wasn't received, but they also don't expect 100% to result in sales, so they might be ok since it's just the cost of doing business. It's also unlikely to be a single address, so how many were impacted? Maybe your response rate is actually pretty good once you exclude the ones that didn't make it through.

What if the mail was about a data breach? You want people to hear it first from you, not from what might be a skewed social media story.

What if it was a product recall? Do you have a legal requirement to reach those people?

What if it was perishable goods? Is a truck driving around trying to find a location and hoping the home office can identify it before the product goes bad, the customer is unhappy, or the company has to prepare a new truckload once the address is known?

Knowing the story of how the data impacts the business is critical.

Bias in Data

We like to think we're not biased. We like to think we know that unconscious bias might slip into our analytics. But what about the data we use? Is it biased? Was it created with bias, and therefore, any analytics we generate from it also have that bias? How ethical are your data and analytics?

In history, there were times when loans would not be given to people of a certain gender or race. Controls should be in place to prevent that from happening now. However, if biased historical data is used to predict the future, you have unknowingly introduced bias to your predictive analytics. Also, is there a subjective component that allows loan approval to be denied for some unquantifiable reason?

Managed correctly, the data is factual. It tells us what happened, whether we like it or not. But, is what happened what we want to happen in the future? Do we want to continue this? Are there any anomalies in the data that make it questionable? For instance, does the current data concentrate on a specific gender and you want to be more inclusive in the future? This is especially critical in medical research where studies predominantly include men, yet women don't always respond in the same manner to the same treatments.

Data management has always been the foundation of data analysis and data science. If you don't know where the data came from and how it was collected, how can you tell how good it is? If you can't trust the data, how can you trust the analytics you generate from the data? Are you using data that has been governed? Do you know where the data came from, who created it, why they created it, and what they did with it? Do you understand what all the data elements mean or are you making an assumption based on the data element name? Do you have all the data or just a subset? Was the data generated in such a way that certain population groups were excluded? Is the quality sufficient for your needs? Are there any privacy issues impacting your use of the data? Are there any things you're not allowed to do with the data?

Think about what data you need and what data you don't need. For instance, some companies choose not to collect certain data (e.g., gender, race) because they don't want to give the appearance that they are misusing data. The opposite of that is that they also don't have the data to detect unconscious bias and prove fairness in their analytics.

Is the data you're using sufficient? Certain records might be thrown out as insufficient if some columns aren't populated. However, is there a reason that those columns weren't populated? Perhaps throwing out those records means you are left with a subset that doesn't fully represent your audience and have introduced bias. Did the data come from people who voluntarily agreed to share their data? If so, there might be a subset of people who were skeptical and, therefore, your bias comes from people choosing to exclude themselves.

Who is developing the analytics, and who is validating them? Are they governed? You want to watch that no one is unconsciously introducing bias into calculations. As the global economy grows and people move around, they may be working in a culture where they weren't educated. Those cultural differences can unknowingly introduce bias. Using governance over analytics should hopefully bring objectivity because of people's different perspectives.

When were your analytics developed? Some companies spend time developing analytics, getting something that works, and then using it repeatedly to monitor activities. However, times change, so it is necessary to regularly monitor the analytics so that they still produce appropriate results.

Analytics are typically not one-time-only activities. They may become analytics that are produced on a regular basis, such as monthly or quarterly. If this is the case, attention needs to be given to continually validate that your analytics are still good. People can become complacent in following what the analytics tell them, but that only works if the analytics are sound and based on sound data.

If you discover bias in your data, it is important to take action. Determine where the bias occurred and what you need to do to remove the bias. Can the issue be resolved and new data generated? Does a new source of the data need to be located? Does the analytic need to change completely because you can't locate a source of unbiased data? However you resolve it, build in a step to monitor the data. If you found bias once, you need to make sure you don't find it again.

Once analytics are generated, you want to take action on what you discovered. However, have you developed something that gives you a fact to follow? If someone tries to interpret the results, bias could again be introduced. Try to construct your analytic algorithms to avoid interpretation. That will help you avoid a subjective component interpreted with bias.

When you consider what you're doing with analytics, also consider ethics. Ethics goes beyond compliance or risk mitigation. The law may not have caught up, so you might have to consider the spirit of the law rather than just the letter of the law. Without official policies, you might have to add guardrails to prevent people from getting into trouble. Are you doing something that you would be comfortable seeing on the front page of the news? Is this something you can defend in open court?

Today, many companies are taking an approach to be proactive in social responsibility. They want a sense of community around issues such as diversity and ideology. Will the analytics produced do any harm? What responsibility does the company have? Is inaction as bad as taking the wrong action?

Build awareness in your data management and data science teams so they understand the concepts of bias and ethics and know what to watch out for. Be completely transparent about where the data comes from and how calculations are performed. There's no good reason to hide information from others.

Data in Real Life—Know Your Data

An employee complained that the data was wrong. His concern was that the sales trend had suddenly fallen, so he assumed the data was bad. After an investigation, no problems were found in the data or the processes that managed the data. All data received was being loaded. No data was erroring out. Everything was good.

He continued his demands that the data was wrong and made more people concerned as he told everyone he knew, so a more formal investigation was launched. After several weeks, the final results were in. The data was correct. There was absolutely nothing wrong with the data he was seeing. However, there was a drop in sales data that coincided with a hurricane. This was a huge event that was covered in national and international media. He could not have missed the event. Due to the seriousness of the hurricane, buildings were destroyed and people relocated. Sales declined because the places they sold to had been demolished and sales reps relocated when their homes were destroyed. If the employee had searched further, he would have seen increased sales in places these sales reps and customers had relocated to.

> Don't just think about data as numbers and letters.
> Data has real meaning and you have to
> understand that meaning if you're going to be
> successful with analytics, or even just a basic
> report.

When the pandemic hit in 2020, lots of data trends changed. We need to consider this as well. 2020 probably had the biggest data trend break people will ever see. Hopefully!

Data in Real Life–Food Pickup Research Project

I accidentally found myself in the midst of a research project.

A place I sometimes order lunch has multiple methods to order–cashier, kiosk, web, and phone app. The method you choose determines how your name appears on the receipt. I get either "Merrill" or "M Albert." The name displayed on the receipt tells the employee what name to yell out. I get either "Merrill" or "Albert." I seem to never get "M Albert." I guess they're ignoring the letter.

Then I discovered something new. If you do Rapid Pick-up, your order is placed in a certain area, so no one yelling names, but now the location of your order is dictated by the employee who placed it there. I often find "M Albert" under "A," but was surprised one day to find "M Albert" under "M."

The volume wasn't big enough to really matter, but think if you do that with your data. If there are multiple places to look for it, you know some places will be missed. Working with the data will be challenging if you can't count on the name or location.

Data in Real Life–Is Technology Making Us Stupid?

A real estate agent set up a client to receive automatic listings based on select criteria. Upon receiving the first set of listings, the client reminded the agent that these didn't meet the criteria.

The agent claimed the application did not allow for the specificity required by the client. While that may be so, shouldn't we actually be looking at the results? If the agent won't curate the results based on the documented criteria, why is there an expectation of a commission?

In this situation, the agent was not the developer and could not fix the application. Even if the agent could, it would not be fixed immediately. That leaves two options–accept the results or use some human intelligence to enhance the results. That's one thing we must keep in mind if the results we get are not what we need. We can't just blame it on technology, especially when we're the ones guiding the technology.

Sixteen

Consulting

There are a lot of consultants out there. I've sometimes been one of them! It is not uncommon for companies to hire a consultant to get started with data management or to help figure out why the company's data management function isn't working properly. If you decide to use consultants, you'll have a contract. This contract will also help you clearly define what you need and what you will get from the consultant. Be realistic. This is your company, so you can't just engage someone to "give" you data management and then leave. They will turn things over for you to keep running in their absence. This also applies if you're engaging in consulting in the form of fractional services.

I've seen good and bad consultants. The good ones have the attitude that they are temporarily helping you. They are not employees and need to train you to take on tasks when they leave. They take pride in their work. They clearly document things for you and leave you without any confusion about what to do next. Then there are the bad ones. The bad ones tend to be secretive. They want to keep things from you so that you will be dependent on them and keep contracting with them indefinitely. They don't want you to understand things enough to take them over. They don't really care that you have good data; they just want you to pay them. Stay away from these consultants.

A good consultant will work with you to help you learn concepts and do tasks. You want someone who understands theory and also has practical knowledge of how to do things and what happens when you don't do them. If someone just understands theory, they might talk a good story but don't practically understand what that means to you. On the other hand, if they don't understand theory, they might have just learned on the job. In this case, they might be able to tell you what they've done in the past, but it might not be the only approach that will work for you.

Communication is important. You want a consultant who can help you and can get points across. You want someone who can clearly explain things. I've seen some consultants who know what needs to be done, but their language isn't resonating with their clients. I've also seen some consultants who put together poor presentations where people get lost in simple things like confusing formats. You don't want to get lost in something simple like PowerPoint or language skills.

Seventeen

Terminology

Some of the terms I use in this book might be what people have heard before and some might be slightly different. People have questioned if the data industry has a common language, or more likely, questioned why it doesn't.

Some people have evolved language on the job to something that works for their employer. Some companies started using language and dug in with its use because it was easier than changing all their marketing and training materials. Some largely volunteer organizations pride themselves on the work they've done. And it is a lot of work! But that doesn't necessarily mean that the organization can speak for everyone. They've had certain experiences and are being generous in sharing their experiences, but it's a subset of people who had time to participate.

211

Think in general about how language evolves. There's sometimes a mostly "official" name for something, but the people speak and the words used can change over time. Within a country, certain words can be very regional. Depending on how you grew up, what you were taught, and what you experienced, your words might differ from someone else's. A language can have many dialects.

Some people are educated through a formal university or college program. Some attend vendor training. Some attend an organization's programs. Some people get certification through an organization, although that isn't equivalent to a university degree program. Some are educated through their employer.

That's a long-winded way of saying there isn't a common language and there doesn't need to be. There are common concepts, and there are different ways you can implement those concepts. Just make sure you understand how the people you interact with use the words so you can talk in a compatible manner.

Reference Data

Some people use the term "reference data." I tend to stay away from this term because it doesn't have a consistent meaning. If people want to use it, I just ask them what it means to them so that we don't have confusion.

At one point, people used the term reference data to mean code values, such as customer type codes of 1, 2, and 3. Those values though are metadata. When master data came along, some people referred to that as reference data, believing that customer data was fairly static and referenced by transaction data. But that's master data. When we can use terms like metadata and master data, I don't see the need to also use reference data.

I feel that "reference data" is a term that has evolved during the life of the data management discipline. I find it easiest to avoid the term because not everyone who uses the term has evolved at the same pace. Like everything, as long as you can agree on a definition, you can talk about it consistently.

Analytics? Data Analytics? Business Analytics?

I talk about analytics, not data analytics. I probably cringe a little when I hear "data analytics." The issue is that if you say "data analytics," you're using a qualifier. You're saying that you have analytics about the data. Do you really? Sometimes, people go very deep into data and develop analytics about the data, but that isn't too common.

When we generally think about analytics, we're trying to take all this data stored in our databases and generate some knowledge from it. It's not for the use of those of us working with data. It's for the use of the business. They want some information that can help them better manage the business. For that reason, I'm fine with people referring to it as "business analytics" rather than just "analytics." If you need a qualifier, or if it helps get the point across about how important analytics are, then say "business analytics," not "data analytics."

The Wheel

The data management discipline is broken up into multiple capabilities. Many people represent this in the form of a wheel.

I've worked in numerous places where each organization had its own data management wheel. There are also organizations that have created their own wheels, which are modified occasionally. Many people use these wheels, either the current version or an older one. If you use someone else's wheel, you have to conform to what they do and potentially pay for the rights to use it, even at all your client sites.

None of the wheels are wrong. I might look at them and see some overlapping areas or wonder where something is, but as long as the people who created them could explain the differences, I could work with it.

I've been hesitant to create my own wheel for the "wheel landscape," but I decided to. However, you'll see that I put it at the end of the book because I didn't want to write a "how to do data management" book. This book was meant to be read for ideas so you could do what works for you. And who knows? Maybe in the future, there might be more of a "how to" book. Maybe that's a cliffhanger.

DATA MANAGEMENT

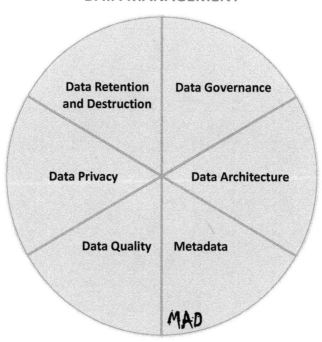

Beyond Data Management

Although this book has been about data management, I have alluded to some other areas that are similar. While we have to keep up with data management, we also have to look to the future and how we can apply these principles to other areas. Some people have already been doing this with information and analytics. We're going to see it more as AI evolves. Let's make AI successful by being ready with the right data and understanding how we're going to manage this new world.

Information Management

Some people practice information management and there are a lot of similarities with data management. Instead of data, you're looking at information, often in the form of documents and content. You need to manage those documents and content. You need to store your documents and content so that you can find them again in the future. You need to understand and follow privacy rules for your documents and content. You need to follow appropriate rules of retention and destruction for those documents and content.

While I won't go into detail on information management, if you can successfully manage data, you should be able to successfully manage information. You're following the same principles.

Analytics Management

While it doesn't have the name recognition of data management and information management, you need to consider analytics management as well. I've designed analytics governance organizations that work similarly to data governance organizations. They often work side-by-side because analytics need data. If the people working on analytics don't understand the data, they won't be as successful as they could be. They're not the data decision makers, but they do need to be informed of the data decisions.

When you're designing analytics, you need to understand the reason behind them. It's not a technical exercise where you code something and then move on to the next exciting project. There's a business reason behind it and you need to understand that business reason. You need business involvement. You need to develop repeatable analytics, meaning you must have them documented. You need to understand the data you're using so you can use it properly. Test everything and make sure the business approves it. You also have to think about maintenance. Data changes over time and that can impact analytics. If you're running the same analytics every month, you might need to look at your calculations on a periodic basis to see if any data changes impact your calculations. You're working your way through very similar decisions as data management, but now you focus on analytics.

AI Management

That brings us to the next big thing—AI. If you haven't figured out the progression yet, similar principles exist with AI as exist with data, information, and analytics.

A lot of what people call AI today is really just a rebranding of what's been going on for years. You go to the fast-food restaurant to place an order on the screen. You order a hamburger and it tries to upsell you a combo meal with fries and a drink. Some people call it AI, but it's been happening for years. Behind the scenes is program code with a bunch of if-then statements. If a hamburger is ordered, then suggest fries and a drink. The cashier used to upsell us in the same manner at the register.

On the other hand, there is more sophisticated AI, where we talk about AI being able to learn. Some things happen, and AI can take action based on those events from what it learned. If the events change, the AI result can change.

Think about what is going into AI. For the most part, we're talking about data and rules. AI is taking action based on the data and rules you gave it. Have you governed the data? Have you governed the rules? If the end result is not what you expect, do you have the rules documented so you can work on figuring out what happened? What would you say if you had to defend what AI did in court?

When an application does something unexpected, it's important to understand why and fix what's wrong. Are the rules wrong? Are the rules right but implemented wrong? What does the documentation say? This still applies in the AI world. You still need accountability. You can't just blame AI. It's usually a human problem. Find the human and find what was wrong so you can fix it so it doesn't happen again.

> One of the things people are very conscious about is being able to use AI to prevent bias. However, if the same rules are going into AI as the rules that humans use that created the bias, we expect AI to learn how to be biased. And we don't want that.

Years ago, people couldn't get a loan if they were of a certain gender or ethnicity. By applying governed rules, that bias can be eliminated. If we hand over loan approval to AI, then AI needs to understand how to apply those unbiased rules or we've stepped backward in history. We need to be conscious that AI is not the savior and can still make bad decisions or even make things up.

You need accountability and traceability. We've already seen cases where something unexpected happened, which results in people trying to explain it without having used any level of governance. Data governance has been able to rein in the chaos and Wild West of working in an ungoverned environment. We hopefully learned from that and can apply a similar level of governance to AI.

Data in Real Life—Crimes Against Humans

After a death in the family, a man needed to take a flight. Using the airline's chatbot, he was told to buy a full price ticket and then submit it afterward for a partial refund for the reduced bereavement rate.

After the funeral and submitting the ticket, the airline informed him that he didn't qualify for the reduced rate on completed travel.

Although he had saved the chatbot discussion, the airline pointed him to a different webpage with contradictory information.

The man sued. The airline claimed the chatbot was "a separate legal entity that is responsible for its own actions."

The airline lost.

This is a great example of how people jump on the AI bandwagon without knowing what it really means. In this case, the airline offered bereavement rates for flights. That's a great thing to offer because after a death, people are often taking a last-minute flight at the maximum price. Rather than wasting time on hold to talk to a human, this man decided to take advantage of the chatbot to understand the rules for bereavement rates. He was smart in saving a copy of the conversation as proof. Had he taken the time to check the depths of the airline's website, he likely would have stumbled across the rules, but it makes sense during a crisis that he didn't have time. He was able to quickly find the information through chat.

The problem the airline created is they used different rules. Their website used the rule that you had to ask for the bereavement rate before travel. Their chatbot used the rule that you could ask for the bereavement rate after travel. The chatbot was on their website; it wasn't a separate entity. The chatbot did not make up its own mind. They programmed the chatbot to tell this man incorrect information. It was appropriate that the airline lost the lawsuit and it's a good reminder to companies not to get swept up in the AI hype cycle.

Data in Real Life—My Car is Making Stuff Up

My car either interprets signs oddly or is challenged with AI. It's supposed to read speed limit signs and display them on the dash.

In reality, what it reads is black and white speed limit signs. If it's something different, like an orange speed limit sign in a construction zone, it won't read it.

My theory was that it read black and white signs with numbers on them, whether they were speed limit signs or not. Then I realized that wasn't the case either. It will sometimes read highway 10 as 10 mph, but it won't read highway 12 as 12 mph.

My next theory was that it read a black and white sign with a number as long as it ended in either 5 or 0. That wasn't right either.

I was on a highway with signs for 50 mph. I noticed that the speed limit on the dash kept flipping between 50 mph and 25 mph. I started paying a bit more attention and realized it was seeing black and white highway 28 signs and converting that to 25 mph. Since the speed limit and highway identification signs alternated, my car had to keep flipping between the two.

Whether we call it AI or coding to interpret character recognition, it lacked intelligence. It might have thought it was smart changing 28 to 25, but it really didn't understand the meaning of 28. We'll probably see more stories like this as work on AI progresses. And let's remember that the "I" is supposed to stand for "intelligence."

About Merrill

I call myself a data person. There was definitely education involved, but I also believe I was born this way. That is why I'm constantly seeing data problems in my daily life and understanding how a company got itself into that mess. Convincing a random help desk representative of the problem can sometimes be difficult, but it eventually gets solved.

Education-wise, it started at the University of Waterloo. I have an Honours Bachelor of Mathematics degree, with a major in Operations Research and a minor in Computer Science. During that program, I learned about good data design. They hadn't yet identified all the capabilities we think of today, but the underlying structure was there, even if the terms weren't. This is also where I learned data modeling from a tool-agnostic view. We weren't constrained by how a tool vendor does something. I could take my knowledge to any vendor, and did.

After graduation, I did what we all did with a BMath degree. I became a programmer/analyst. Although it wasn't my ultimate dream, it does give street credibility. Although I only did it for a couple of years, it did help me experience the problems developers face when they don't have good data to work with. From there, I got a job as a data modeler, then data architect, and then the world of data management was wide open to me. For the most part, my specialty has been data governance, where I govern all the data management capabilities, so this pulls everything related to data altogether.

As new developments came along in the data field, people often turned to me to figure it out. In most cases, these concepts, while new in name, were not new to me in what I was doing. Data governance was a new concept, but at the same time, I had been doing a form of it when I was data modeling. I had to because I had to juggle people from across the company telling me what they thought the data was for and what it meant. I had to bring people together and negotiate deals. MDM came along and I realized I had been doing that too. While I didn't have fancy tools, I had to architecturally design it and build the data rules because those fancy tools hadn't been invented yet.

Now, I help companies understand what data management means, what problems they have because of it, and how they can implement it. The goal is to better manage your data to drive value from it.

Index

www.ingramcontent.com/pod-product-compliance
Lightning Source LLC
Chambersburg PA
CBHW071240050326
40690CB00011B/2206